The Life and Death of Floyd Collins

The Life and Death of Floyd Collins

by
HOMER COLLINS
as told to
JOHN LEHRBERGER

CAVE BOOKS

Copyright © 2001 by Cave Research Foundation
The original manuscript of this book was transcribed in 1955.
All rights reserved. This book or parts thereof may not be reproduced in any form without permission.

Published by CAVE BOOKS
4700 Amberwood Drive, Dayton, OH 45424
CAVE BOOKS is the publications affiliate of the Cave Research Foundation.

Cover photo: Floyd Collins on the entrance steps to Crystal Cave. Photo by Russell T. Neville. CRF Collection.
Frontispiece: Floyd's final resting place in the Grand Canyon of Crystal Cave. Photo by Roger E. McClure.

Layout and page makeup by William Mixon.
Cover graphic design by Gary Berdeaux.
Publishing and production by Roger McClure.

Library of Congress Cataloging-in-Publication Data

Collins, Homer, 1901-
  The life and death of Floyd Collins / by Homer Collins as told to John Lehrberger.
    p. cm.
  ISBN 0-939748-39-8, 978-0-939748-39-6 (hardback : alk. paper) -- ISBN 0-939748-47-9, 978-0-939748-47-1 (pbk. : alk. paper) 1. Collins, Floyd, 1890-1925. 2. Speleologists--Kentucky--Biography. 3. Sand Cave (Ky.)--Discovery and exploration. I. Lehrberger, John. II. Title.

GB601.6.C64C65 2005
796.52'5'092--dc22

2005006326

Printed in the United States of America.

CONTENTS

    Publisher's Note *7*
    Preface *9*
1. In the Hills of Old Kentucky *11*
2. Indian Remains *19*
3. Buzzard's Roost *35*
4. Donkey's Cave *47*
5. Edmund Turner *55*
6. The Great Discovery *67*
7. Great Crystal Cave *81*
8. Helictite Gallery *91*
9. Cave War *99*
10. The Lower Levels *105*
11. Floyd's Lost Passage *115*
12. Sand Cave *121*
13. Trapped *129*
14. The Rescue Begins *139*
15. The Rescue Continues *155*
16. The Shaft *171*
17. The Inquiry *181*
18. The Race Against Time *189*
19. Floyd's Mausoleum *199*

A NOTE FROM THE PUBLISHER

Forty-six years have passed since this book was written, and seventy-five to over a hundred years have passed since the events described herein took place. Both were times of cave wars, when rival owners of commercial caves competed for tourists. Cave formations, Indian artifacts, and even blind fish were openly taken from the caves to be sold. And a strong man thought nothing of descending or ascending a pit hand-over-hand on a rope. Grand tales were told to enhance the attraction of the caves and the souvenirs sold to tourists.

So perhaps you should not believe everything that Homer told Jack, and you are earnestly implored not to go caving or treat the objects and formations in caves as did Floyd Collins. This is not to fault Floyd. He was a man, even a giant of a man, of his age, and he will always remain a hero to cavers for his exploits exploring alone underground. But Floyd's time began in the nineteenth century and ended only a quarter of the way through the twentieth.

We are at the beginning of the twenty-first century, and we have learned that caves are fragile in many ways. Their features take hundreds or thousands of years to form. Cave animals such as blind fish are rare, and they always live in precarious ecological balance in their underground environments. Cave features and cave life can be destroyed unknowingly by people who enter caves without informing themselves about cave conservation. Great, irreparable damage has been done by people who take stalactites and other flowstone features from caves or disturb cave life such as bats, which are especially vulnerable in winter when they are hibernating. Prehistoric people left artifacts, their bones, and even their footprints in many caves. These are precious records that should not be disturbed. Caves are wonderful places for scientific research and recreational adventure, but before you enter a cave please first learn about careful caving by contacting the National Speleological Society, 2813 Cave Avenue, Huntsville, Alabama 35810.

PREFACE

On February 13, 1954, forty cave explorers assembled in central Kentucky to conduct an expedition into Floyd Collins Crystal Cave, which later proved to be part of the most extensive cave system in the world. On their way down into this complex maze, in a passage called the Grand Canyon, they walked past a coffin containing the remains of Floyd Collins, America's most famous cave explorer. Their objective was to establish a base camp deep underground in Floyd's Lost Passage from which they would try to extend the discoveries of that solitary caver. For a week they explored and mapped the lower levels of Floyd Collins Crystal Cave, supported by a steady stream of supplies dragged in from the surface by special support teams. Staying below the ground the entire week to report this story to the world was the same man who had won the Pulitzer prize in 1925 for his coverage of the Floyd Collins tragedy. This man was Skeets Miller, the reporter who had turned rescue worker and risked his life to help save Floyd Collins.

Floyd Collins had discovered a key part of the great cave system and explored it single-handedly, often staying underground for days at a time alone. Until this expedition, the public knew of him only as the man who was trapped and died in Sand Cave in 1925, when the whole world was stirred by the dramatic efforts to rescue him. But this man, who wandered in silence through the vast caverns, was also one of history's great adventurers and played a vital role in the exploration of the world's longest cave.

This is the story of his life and death as related to me by Homer Collins, Floyd's youngest brother and constant companion.

John Lehrberger, 1955

ONE

In the Hills of Old Kentucky

EXPLORER TRAPPED IN CAVE! In the year 1925—thirty years ago—the headline flashed across the newspapers of the nation. There have been many catastrophes in which hundreds of men were trapped underground. None ever received the attention that was given to my brother, Floyd Collins. The lone cave explorer was trapped, his leg caught in a rock vise at the edge of a pit far beneath the surface of the earth in Sand Cave in central Kentucky. He was slowly being tortured to death in a dark crevice whose rock walls dripped icy water. Cave explorers, miners, engineers, college professors—men from every walk of life—tried to save him. The odds were overwhelmingly against them. Nevertheless, unable to move, covered with muck, and at the mercy of the wet, penetrating cold, Floyd never gave up hope.

I have been asked many times why we were unable to rescue Floyd. People also ask me what sort of man he was to spend days alone exploring underground, completely cut off from the world above, with a few cans of beans to feed himself. The answer lies in the story of my brother's life. Floyd, fifteen years older than I, was like a father to me. In my childhood, I trailed after him like a puppy dog, and later we worked together in the cave business. He pioneered the exploration of the greatest cave system in the world, and I accompanied him on many of his explorations.

We lived in a log cabin built by our father, Lee Collins. It was located near the Green River about four miles east of Mammoth Cave. William Floyd Collins was born in this cabin on June 20, 1887. He was the third child of Martha Collins, who gave birth to eight children: Elizabeth, James, Floyd, Annie, Andy Lee, Marshall, Nellie, and Homer. I was the youngest child, and there are only three of us still living today [1955]. Nellie and I live in Louisville. Marshall lives in Horse Cave, Kentucky. He has a small factory in his back yard where he cuts and polishes cave onyx to make souvenirs.

At the time Floyd was born, Pap (as we called our father) had no thought of entering the cave business, although he was sitting on top of one of the most beautiful caves in the world. Pap was a farmer and he did not realize that the true value of his property lay beneath the soil, for the gypsum-covered passages of Crystal Cave had not yet been discovered.

Our farm was located in rugged hill country. There were few surface streams in the region, as the water drains off underground through the caves. The Green River, the main stream in that part of the country and base level for the caves that empty into it, has cut a steep-walled valley through the area. When Floyd was a child, the river bluffs were covered with virgin timber. The woods had once abounded in game. There were deer, bear, wolves, and even panthers. These big cats are known by different names in various parts of the country: cougar, puma, mountain lion, catamount, panther, or "painter." Floyd heard them many times at night in the woods around our farm. "They had a peculiar yell," he told me, "like the sound of a woman crying."

When Floyd was four or five years old, he used to run to Pap shouting, "Get the gun, the painters are near!" On one occasion, Pap heard a noise in the barn and when he rushed out to see what was wrong, he found a panther trying to get at one of our calves.

When Floyd was about six years old, he met one of these cats. Our house was located just a short distance from the Green River bluffs, and water had to be carried from a spring near Buzzards Cave about a hundred yards away. One night, Floyd and my brother Jim were sent down to the spring for a bucket of water. Floyd was walking in front with a lard-oil lamp lighting the way for Jim, who carried the bucket. They walked down the narrow path through the woods to the edge of the bluff. From there, the path winds down the hill a short distance and then runs alongside some vertical rock walls. As the two boys approached the spring, Jim was suddenly terrified by the sight of two eyes on a ledge over Floyd's head. "They was like two balls of fire," Jim said.

There was a panther crouched on the ledge. Floyd had not noticed the cat, for he was watching the path. Jim dropped the bucket and yelled at Floyd. Floyd looked up and saw the eyes gleaming directly above his head. If the panther decided to spring, Floyd was finished. In the meantime, Jim continued yelling, too scared to move. Floyd froze in his tracks, still holding onto the lamp. Then suddenly the panther turned and disappeared in the darkness. The boys did not run back to the house immediately, but went to the spring to get the water. The panther did not appear again and they made it back to the house with no harm done.

Floyd used to spend much of his time roaming the bluffs along the Green River. Sometimes he gathered ginseng for Mother. Ginseng is a medicinal herb, and Mother used it to make a medicine she called bitters. She had tuberculosis and this medicine gave her some relief. Another herb she used was yellow root. I do not know the exact formula, except that she mixed the herbs with whiskey. One day as Floyd was out looking for ginseng, he noticed a hole in the face of the cliff up above him and decided to take a look inside. He was able to reach it by climbing about six feet up the vertical wall. Clinging to the rocks, he poked his head inside the hole for a preliminary look. At first, he could see nothing, but his eyes gradually became accustomed to the dim light. He squirmed forward until his entire body was inside, then he lay still, peering into the darkness. His heels were just inside the opening—about as far as he cared to go without a light. As he lay there in the semi-darkness, two shiny beads suddenly confronted him. Once again, Floyd was face to face with a panther. Floyd rose to his knees terrified. There was not room enough for him to stand up. He took the only possible course, backpedaling toward the entrance as fast as he could move. He came scooting out feet first and without stopping to climb down the six feet of rock wall below the opening, slid over the edge and fell to the ground all in one motion.

From his position on the ground, he looked up just in time to see the panther leap out of the hole and into a tree a few feet away. Floyd and the cat took off at top speed in opposite directions. This convinced Floyd that he should not go poking his head into any more holes without first looking for animal tracks.

On his way home, Floyd began thinking how easy it would be to hide near the panther's den and plug the cat when it came out. Pap would not allow him to carry firearms as Floyd was only ten years old at the time. But Floyd was determined to get that panther. During the next few days, he could not get it out of his mind. Every time he saw Pap's old musket hanging on the wall, his desire to kill the cat grew stronger. He knew Pap would not give him permission to use the musket, so he decided to borrow it on the sly. He hung around the house waiting for an opportunity. Finally, when no one was in the house, he grabbed the musket and headed for the river.

Near the den, he found a ledge overlooking the entrance. From that point, he could watch without being seen. He sat down, propped up the musket, and waited. Hours passed, but the panther did not appear. He waited in silence throughout the day without moving from the spot. Toward evening, the cat finally came out. Floyd was trembling—what if he missed and the panther charged? The cat was crouched at the edge of the hole with only his head showing. Slowly Floyd squeezed the trigger. The old musket fired. The cat stood still for a few seconds, then disappeared inside the den. Floyd waited, but the panther did not come out again. Rather than take the chance on being caught by the cat in the darkness, Floyd left his post and returned home. He replaced the musket and said nothing to anyone.

The panther was still on the loose and Floyd was more determined than ever to kill it. He decided that the next time he would use Pap's good rifle instead of the musket. At the first opportunity, he eased the rifle out of the house and once more set off to kill the panther. Floyd approached the area cautiously, seated himself on the ledge, and prepared for a long wait. Again it was toward evening before the cat made its appearance. Floyd took careful aim—there must be no mistake this time. He pulled the trigger and the cat leaped into the air. It rolled a short distance down the hillside and thrashed about in the underbrush. Then the panther got to its feet and began limping down the river bank in the direction of our farm. Floyd followed along behind to make sure that it did not escape wounded. The panther stopped frequently as it ran along the river bank, so Floyd was able to keep it in sight. He had reached a position about fifty feet from the panther on the uphill side when it suddenly turned on him. At that point the hillside was almost vertical. Although the cat was badly wounded, it was still capable of doing a lot of damage. The slope was covered with loose rocks and boulders. Floyd, frantic at the sight of the approaching panther, began kicking rocks down the hillside. Some of the rocks, which were quite large, struck the cat with great force. One boulder sent it reeling down the slope where it was finally stopped by a tree trunk. Now it lay still, but Floyd sent down several small avalanches just to make sure. After waiting several minutes, he carefully approached to see if the panther was really dead. After making sure of that, he began to wonder what he should do with the carcass. If Pap found out that he had taken the rifle from the house without asking permission, he would get a good licking. Floyd decided to roll the panther into the river. The chase had taken him downstream to a point directly above Pike Spring. He rolled the cat down the hillside and into the channel where the underground river flows out from under the hill. Then Floyd returned home and put the rifle back in its place. Later, he became a

Floyd Collins as a young boy. *Photo from Howard W. Hartley's* Tragedy of Sand Cave.

very good hunter and had a reputation for being a good shot, but this was his most exciting kill.

Floyd's first contact with cave tragedy came when he was only ten years old. In the year 1897, an entrance was being dug into Great Salts Cave just across the valley from our farm. It consisted of a vertical shaft that entered the ground at the base of a sandstone bluff near the top of the ridge. The cave itself was perfectly safe inside, but there was a lot of loose rock around the shaft. A stairway had not yet been built, so the workers were being hauled up and down with a windless.

One of the men working on the shaft was called Pike Chapman. A local cave explorer, he used to stop by our house frequently on his way to the Green River where he often fished. We called him Pike because he spent so much time fishing at Pike Spring, a subterranean river that entered into the Green River just below our farm.

Pike Chapman was being hauled out of the shaft when a rock came loose at the top and fell, striking him on the head. Most cave explorers now wear hard hats, but Pike did not. He was brought out bleeding profusely. The men immediately sent out a call for help. Pap, Floyd, and my oldest brother Jim heard the cries from across the valley and ran over to see what had happened.

Pike Chapman was carried to Dr. Hazen's house, while Floyd was sent on the run for outside help. It was too late for help. Pike Chapman died. The shaft in which he was killed became known as Pike Chapman's Entrance. The memory stayed with Floyd, but it did not frighten him away from caves. Years later he was to work in that same shaft himself.

TWO

Indian Remains

Pap raised chickens on the farm, and sold eggs to the Mammoth Cave Hotel. From the time that Floyd was old enough to hang on behind Pap on the horse, he went along on these trips to the hotel. It was like a visit to the big city for Floyd, although to the tourists who visited there it seemed like a remote outpost of civilization. Mammoth Cave was already quite famous at that time. People came from all over the world to see this "wonder of the world." Little did anyone suspect, least of all Floyd, that he himself would someday discover as great a wonder and guide people through it.

While Pap transacted business at the hotel, Floyd watched the tourists with great interest. Their dress, manners, and speech seemed strange to him, so different from what he knew.

Floyd soon discovered that these people were fascinated by things that were commonplace to him. They offered him coins in exchange for the stones that he picked up in the fields and carried around in his pockets. As a result of this his pockets soon

Artifacts from Salts Cave.
Photo by Russell T. Neville. CRF Collection.

bulged with rocks as he rode along behind Pap on the way to the hotel. There were also a great many flints, arrowheads, and other Indian relics lying around in the fields and on the bluffs near home. Floyd scoured the area for articles the tourists were eager to buy.

At the age of six, Floyd had begun to wander alone into caves in search of Indian relics. Near our farm there was a cave that had been used by prehistoric men—Great Salts Cave. With only lard-oil lamp to light the way, he went into Salts Cave in search of artifacts among the huge boulders that made up the floor of the main passage. The light from a lard-oil lamp barely penetrated the blackness.

Floyd was too young to realize the dangers that

surrounded him. He did not have a smooth path to walk on as tourists do now. There were only mountains of rock, boulders weighing many tons, some of them delicately balanced. One mistake and he could have been crushed, perhaps buried in an avalanche of rock, never to be found. More than one Indian had been mummified in the dry passages, to be found centuries later by explorers such as Floyd. There were pits and crevices where a slip would have been fatal. Or he might have dropped his lamp into one of those holes. Without light, he could not have moved in such a cave. Somehow Floyd survived these childhood excursions without mishap.

Very close to home, on top of the Green River bluffs, there were some large sandstone outcrops. In several places on these sandstone rocks, Floyd found smooth cup-shaped holes of various sizes. These holes, a few inches in diameter and as much as a foot deep, had been made by the Indians for grinding corn. Floyd also found sandstone pestles nearby. They were about ten inches long, rounded, and tapered from one end to the other. The Indians had placed corn in the holes and pounded it with

Mummy found in Salts Cave in 1876.
Photo by Russell T. Neville. CRF Collection.

the pestles. It was their crude way of grinding corn.

The Indians obtained their flint from veins found in the limestone outcrops along the bluffs. They made their arrowheads and other implements from this material. Flint is a very hard rock, and Floyd used to wonder how the Indians had shaped it so well. He found pieces lying around that had been chipped off in the shaping process. Also along the bluffs he found the remains of Indian fireplaces in the rock shelters beneath the ledges. Oftentimes the rocks were charred black.

Throughout his childhood Floyd played among the remains of this lost civilization, following the trails of the vanished Indians through the woods and even inside the caves. He often roamed the woods by himself, climbed the river bluffs, and fished along its banks. He knew every inch of the ground in the area, every tree, and every cave hole. He found friendship in the woods that other children feared, and adventure in the caves that were taboo to other boys his age.

Floyd received his formal education at the one-room, one-teacher Mammoth Cave School, a few miles from home. It was open only six months out of the year, from the Fourth of July until Christmas, since the students had many chores to do on the farm.

After finishing the fourth grade, Floyd had to quit school because of his duties on the farm, but later he returned to attend night classes for adults. He was very eager to learn. Wade Highbaugh, a well-known photographer at Mammoth Cave, taught these classes. Floyd went to night school at the age of twenty-three and again when he was thirty-six. He was very fond of reading, and his favorite book was the Bible. I saw him many times reading the Bible by firelight on winter evenings.

In the year 1902, Pap decided to try his luck out west. He was going to homestead in the Durant Indian territory, which later became part of the state of Oklahoma. Mother did not want to go, but Pap had his mind set. In July of 1902, Pap took my brothers Andy Lee and Marshall with him and set out for Oklahoma, while Floyd stayed with Mother on the farm. I was born in September of that year. In November, Mother gathered the rest of the family together and set out to join Pap in the Durant Territory.

Pap had not yet built a house, so we had to live in tents. Mother was very unhappy about the new home, especially since it was in Indian territory. She could not forget the stories she had been told about wild savages who roamed the country throughout the West. The men drank a good deal around the camp and at night there was a lot of whooping and yelling. Poor Mother could not sleep. After a few weeks, she persuaded Pap to leave the Durant Territory. In the month of December, we returned to the farm in Kentucky. Floyd brought a sprout of a pecan tree back with him and planted it near the house. That sprout is now a beautiful tree, and the tourists visiting Crystal Cave spread their picnic lunches in its shade.

Several years after our return from Oklahoma, we met an old Indian chief from the Choctaw Nation. Pap had gone over to Mammoth Cave to sell eggs, and Floyd was with him selling arrowheads to tourists. I was seven years old at the time, and, as usual, was tagging along behind Floyd. Floyd saw the old Indian outside the hotel and struck up a conversation with him. In broken English, he told Floyd he was a chief in the Choctaw Nation and had become a rich man when oil was found on his land. He leased the land, and although in his eighties, began touring the country. He said he remembered meeting a man from Kentucky out in the Durant Territory—a man who lived in the cave country. As it turned out, Pap had met the chief in 1902, during our brief stay out west.

Floyd told the chief all about the Indian relics around home and in the caves. He described the area along the river bluffs, with its supply of flint, remains of Indian fireplaces, and the sand rocks where the Indians had ground corn. He asked him how the Indians had shaped arrowheads out of the hard flint. The chief explained to Floyd that flint was too hard to grind into shape, so other methods had to be used. One method was very interesting. The flint was first placed in the fire, then when it became very hot, cold water was dripped on it. The sudden cooling caused the flint to crack and as a result small chips would fly off. In this way they were able to shape the hard flint without actually cutting it.

Immediately Floyd pictured what must have happened on the bluffs. He recalled the fireplaces on the ledges where the flint was found and the many odd pieces lying around that had evidently turned out badly in the chipping process. Everything fitted neatly together. They must have used the cold water from the spring that flowed out of the hillside near by. Floyd remarked, "It was an Indian arrowhead factory, and they didn't have to import their flint."

Floyd was always interested in the Indians who had inhabited the region. Throughout his life he sought for clues to the nature of the lost civilization, clues that had been hidden for centuries, well preserved inside the caves. He was hunting for the parts of a historical jigsaw puzzle that has not yet been fully pieced together.

One day when Floyd was twelve years old and selling flints to the tourists at Mammoth Cave, he met a young geologist from Buffalo, New York. The man's name was Edmund Turner. Floyd had asked him if he wanted to buy any arrowheads. Turner bought some from him and then asked if he knew of any other Indian artifacts. Floyd answered that he could find many other Indian relics as well as arrowheads, even some tomahawks. He told Turner that he knew a cave where he could get Indian moccasins in perfect shape. Turner promised to pay him well for these moccasins and gave him an address in New York to which he could mail them. With this, Floyd began entering the caves in earnest. It was the biggest factor in launching him into cave exploration. Plain old curiosity might have done just as well, but this gave him an early start. He had been going into caves since the age of six, so now at twelve he was not exactly a beginner. His search for Indian relics made caving a routine task—a lonely one for a young boy.

The cave Floyd had in mind when he told Turner he could find Indian moccasins was Great Salts Cave, one of the largest in the region. Some Indian mummies had been removed from it previously, and its corridors were littered with Indian relics. It was given the name Great Salts because of the snowy white formations that hung from the walls and ceiling of the passages and accumulated in thick beds on the floor. The formations were made of magnesium sulfate—plain old Epsom salts. There was one room in Salts Cave where the heat from a lantern would cause flakes of white salt to fall from the ceiling like sparkling snow. Although he had been in this cave many times before and had seen the moccasins lying about, they were so commonplace that he had not attached much value to them. Now he began to search for them in earnest.

Pieces of gourds, squash, and spear from Salts Cave. *Photo by Russell T. Neville. CRF Collection.*

The morning after meeting Turner, Floyd set out for Great Salts Cave carrying an old grease lamp with him for light. These lamps burned lard oil and were used in the old days by the guides at Mammoth Cave before they began using kerosene and gas lanterns. The lamp Floyd had with him was one that had been discarded at Mammoth Cave. He used to pick up these lamps and fix them for his own use. They were simple and dependable lights. A pot held about one pint of oil with a wick sticking out of it. The pot was suspended by four wires twisted together at the top to form a handle. In extremely tight crawlways, the wires could be bent down so the lamp could be shoved through.

Floyd walked a mile and a half to the entrance to the cave. The entrance is at the bottom of a huge sinkhole some two hundred feet in diameter and fifty feet deep. These sinkholes are typical of cave country. They are roughly conical shaped depressions in the ground ranging from a few feet to a hundred yards or more in diameter. They have walls all around, the only drainage being at the bottom where the water runs off underground. Sometimes they become clogged with debris that falls in from the sides, but occasionally there is an opening through which one can enter the underlying cave passage. Often the opening leads to a pit that may drop a hundred feet or more to the cave below. Fortunately for Floyd, no such vertical shaft led off from the bottom of this sink. On one side of the sink at the entrance to Great Salts Cave, a spring gushes out from a cavity in the rocks and sinks into the ground without any visible opening. It comes from no one knows where and goes to a similar place. On the opposite side, another spring flows out of a small passage near the top of the sinkhole and cascades over the rocks forming a waterfall as it pours over a ledge near the bottom. This waterfall drops into an opening and disappears in a mountain of loose rock that slopes down a hundred feet to the floor of the cave.

Floyd scrambled down the hillside and stood beside the waterfall peering into the darkness below. He began the descent into the cave by moving very slowly, for even with his lamp he could not at first see any farther than the rocks on which he placed his feet. It took some time for his eyes to become adjusted to the dim light after leaving daylight behind. At the base of the slope, he walked past two large, flat rocks weighing several tons each that had fallen from the ceiling in times past to stand on edge buried deeply in the floor like axe blades in a block of wood. Turning around, Floyd could see the opening far above him with the sunlight shining through the curtain of water that falls in at the entrance. The mountain of loose rock inside was dimly lit by the rays. The waterfall sounded like a heavy rain pouring down outside. Floyd lingered for a moment—he never tired of this sight. But there was work to do, so he turned his back to the sunlight and headed into the darkness. He climbed to the top of a hill of rock that rose all the way to the ceiling and passed through a small opening at the top. Now he was in big cave. The sound of the waterfall no longer reached his ears and he could no longer see the sunlight filtering in the entrance. He was in an enormous passage, walking with difficulty over great blocks of limestone piled to a depth of fifty or sixty feet. His lamp was as important to him as the air he breathed, for in this type of cave his life depended on his light—no movement was possible without it.

Few grown men would have entered this cave alone as Floyd did as a child. It is not merely the fear of getting lost or falling that makes a big cave frightening to a lone explorer, for these things are easily avoided by using a little care. There is something else about a big, wild cave—something intangible, yet very real. Imagine yourself surrounded by blocks of stone, many as large as a house. The blackness around you is like a fluid mass that gives way to your light and immediately closes in again behind it. With every step your supply of light diminishes, and the darkness has plenty of time to wait. The silence is depressing. It lets you listen to your own heartbeat when you stop to rest. A drop of water striking the floor becomes a falling rock. A rivulet becomes a torrent, a small waterfall turns into a roaring Niagara. You stop and listen. Anything that you listen for, you will hear—footsteps, voices, the rumble of rocks. As you walk over the loose rocks, they move, then settle again after you pass. The sound of their settling gives the illusion that someone is following you. You become tense. You want to look behind, but you must not. There are eyes watching from the ledges overhead, peering from behind every boulder. Shadows leap across the passage in the flickering light. You do not whistle in the dark, for it only makes you more aware of your loneliness. You must keep moving and not look back. You must realize that the source of the sounds and motions that you hear, see, and fancy is you. A lone caver is the loneliest of animals.

Floyd felt all these things, but managed to overcome his natural fear. He had been doing this

throughout his childhood. Now he was searching for something and his mind was occupied. In years of caving alone, he had become familiar with the tricks that a cave will play on the eyes and ears. To Floyd, caving was a calculated risk, and he was willing to take that risk.

Floyd walked through a large passage whose walls and ceiling were black with smoke from Indian torches. There were burned reeds lying on the floor. The Indians had carried them into the cave and burned them for light. They had gathered the reeds along the banks of Green River and tied them together with fibers to make torches. Even today, these reeds can be found in great numbers throughout the cave. But Floyd was not interested in reeds, he was looking for moccasins. He did not have to go very far to find them. After passing through the narrow opening at the top of the slope just a short distance inside the entrance, Floyd stopped beside a block of limestone about the size of a wall in your living room. There were many reeds lying on top of this rock and the remains of fireplaces around its edge. Floyd got down on his hands and knees to look underneath. He found a moccasin in nearly perfect shape hidden under the edge of the rock. He picked it up with great care, for after hundreds of years in the cave these moccasins fall apart very easily. He lay on his stomach for a better look under the rock. Just within reach he found a tomahawk. Floyd decided that he had found a good spot so he began moving the smaller rocks away from the edge of the

Moccasin or woven slipper found in cave.
U. S. Museum of Natural History, Smithsonian Institution

big one and crawled underneath. It was a tight squeeze, but he dug his way like a mole and found a string of beads. He wondered if there was an Indian mummy under this rock. He wanted to dig farther, but he knew he had already gone beyond the limit of safety, so he backed out cautiously from under the rock.

After satisfying himself that there was no more to be found around this rock, Floyd moved on deeper into the cave. It occurred to him that the best articles had probably been picked up by others who had scoured the cave long before him. But maybe they had not looked too hard in the out-of-the-way places. Perhaps they had just picked up the ones that were easy to find. There was a chance that no one had really searched under the rocks, in the crevices, the crawlways, and the remote passages. So Floyd began to enter the more difficult places. He found that the Indians had been no slouches when it came to going into rough spots. Wherever he went he found the infallible evidence of Indians' presence, burned reeds and charred rocks.

After having spent many hours in the cave looking for moccasins, he suddenly realized that his supply of oil was low. He was eager to go on searching, but he knew he must get out of the cave before his oil supply gave out. He had to allow himself plenty of time, for he was carrying quite a load of Indian relics, which slowed him down. By the time he reached the entrance, he was on his last drop of oil. The sound of the waterfall was a great relief after the hours of silence. He stopped for a drink at the spring outside, then headed for home with his valuable load.

Floyd received as much as twenty dollars for

some of the specimens he sent to Edmund Turner—big money for a boy at that time. During the next few years he made many more trips alone into Great Salts Cave looking for moccasins and other artifacts. He spent more and more time underground until soon he knew every rock in the main passage. Gradually his search took him into more remote places. He began to wonder just how extensive the cave was, whether there might be other levels than those he had seen, undiscovered passages yet to be found. He began to give more of his attention to the exploration of the cave as he searched for Indian artifacts.

Floyd was no longer content merely to walk along the beaten path. His curiosity drove him in search of new cave. A hole in the wall high above the floor might be a small passage leading to unknown parts of the cave. He climbed up on ledges and squirmed into every opening that he could find. More often than not, he found a dead end. The passage might be filled with broken rocks or with sand that was deposited by streams in ages past, or it might get smaller and smaller until he could no longer force his body through. He went down into deep crevices in search of lower levels. Sometimes he found himself in a side passage that ran beside the main passage for a short distance and then entered it again, sometimes after having crossed under it to enter from the opposite side, which is very confusing. Sometimes he would find himself in a pit with no place to go but back up.

Floyd and Edmund Turner corresponded regularly for a few years, but then Turner stopped writing. Floyd was greatly disappointed, but he continued caving and searching for Indian relics. Exploration became an obsession with him. His greatest thrill came from finding virgin cave passages where no man had ever walked, beauty that had been hidden for millions of years. He found the thrill of discovery more rewarding than the money he received for the Indian relics. Exploration was hard work and sometimes dangerous. It meant leaving behind much of the fun other young men enjoyed, but it was real adventure.

Floyd realized that Flint Ridge, where our home and Great Salts Cave were, had tremendous potential. Now that he was primarily interested in exploration, Floyd set himself a goal. He explained it this way. "We're on a big ridge here—bigger than the Mammoth Cave Ridge. There ought to be a bigger cave under it than Mammoth Cave. If there is, I'm going to find it."

Many years later he did find what he was looking for—Crystal Cave. It is still being explored even today.

THREE

Buzzard's Roost

Floyd's favorite stomping ground was the area around the Green River. Our house was only a hundred yards from the river bluffs. Several hundred feet below, the river snakes its way westward, meandering out of sight between the hills. Pike Spring, one of the main drainage outlets of Flint Ridge, issues from under the hillside nearby. This underground river pours out a never-ending supply of cool, clear water the year around. It is possible to row a boat for a short distance into the cave passage from which the spring issues. The entrance presents a mysterious view to fishermen passing by on the Green River. None that I know have stopped to investigate the black opening barely visible through the foliage.

From the top of a bluff, a path winds down the hill for a few feet, then turns upstream, following a ledge along the limestone outcrop. On one side of the path, the sheer rock wall rises up. On the other side, there is a nearly vertical slope to the water's edge. The hillside across the river is dotted with evergreens. A shout sets up echoes between the valley walls. In the summer, the valley is a world of green that is reflected by the river. In the winter, the water is sometimes hidden under a fog that fills the valley like a huge white river. On a cold, clear, moonlit night, the fog seems thick enough to walk on.

The path leads to a large opening in the cliff wall. This opening, thirty feet wide by fifteen feet high, is the entrance to a cave. The passage narrows inside to three feet in width, then opens again into a room filled with travertine formations: stalactites, stalagmites, and columns. (Travertine is called onyx in the cave region. True onyx is a siliceous mineral, whereas cave onyx is actually calcium carbonate, the same thing that limestone rock is made from. Following the practice of the cave region, I use the term onyx in place of travertine.) On one side of this room is a dome. The walls of the dome are covered with flowstone, an onyx formation deposited in much the same way as stalactites, although it looks as though it had solidified while flowing down the wall in a molten state. At the far end of the room, a crawlway leads to unknown parts of the cave.

The many-spired formations and columns in the cave led to the name Cathedral Cave. Originally, it was called Buzzards Cave. The buzzards roosted there and in the rock shelters nearby. Floyd used to climb up to their nests to steal eggs. Sometimes he would take one of the eggs home and place it under a hen. When the egg hatched there was a mighty surprised hen. He also tried this with hawks' eggs, causing considerable turmoil among the chickens.

There were a lot of cave holes in this area of the bluffs. One day Floyd went down to look at a crawlway that had not been explored. My brother

Marshall, eight years old, tagged along behind him. The crawlway was just large enough for Floyd to get his body through. He lay on his belly and squirmed forward with Marshall at his heels anxious not to lose sight of big brother. They came to a place where the floor of the crawlway was covered with a thin crust of onyx. Floyd crawled over this spot lying flat, while Marshall was able to get through on his hands and knees. Floyd's weight was spread out, with only the toes of his boots digging into the floor with any appreciable force. He noticed that his boots were breaking through the crust, but thought nothing of it, for he had had this happen many times before. Marshall came crawling along behind, unaware that Floyd had weakened the floor so it could no longer support much weight. His knees broke through the crust and he became panicky. If such a crust is over the top of a high, narrow canyon passage and gives way, the explorer can be plunged onto jagged rocks below. Marshall thought this was happening to him. He scrambled forward, but with each move his knees broke through the crust.

"Help me, Floyd! I'm falling through!" he shouted.

"I can't turn around here," Floyd answered. "Keep still and I'll back up to where you can grab onto my boots."

Marshall had little to fear. Actually there were only a few inches separating the crust from the passage floor. Neither Marshall nor Floyd knew this. Floyd came backing down the crawlway feet first as rapidly as possible. Marshall nearly crawled over the top of him when they met.

"Are you all right, Marshall?"

"I ain't hurt none, Floyd."

"Well you sure sound scared. With all that yelling I thought you was gone for sure."

"It felt like the ground was giving way."

"It's just an old onyx crust formed over the dirt. Now don't be scared, just stick close behind me."

Marshall was more in favor of leaving, but he stayed with Floyd. The passage was too small for Floyd to turn around. It began to look as though he would have to back out feet-first if the passage came to an end. (Of all the forms of cave locomotion, crawling backward while lying on one's belly is probably the most discouraging.) Just when it seemed that the crawlway was going to pinch out, it opened into a small room. The walls were covered with drapery, an onyx formation that hangs in thin sheets like petrified drapery. Floyd held his light behind the formations and found that they were translucent, giving an orange glow. Floyd could not find any other passages leading out of the room, so they started back through the crawlway. This time Marshall acted as if he were crawling over egg shells. His desire to be an explorer was left behind in the crawlway, but he was one experience wiser in the ways of caving.

Floyd was very much interested in Buzzards Cave. There was one crawlway that he felt would lead to big cave. When the passage became too small to squeeze through, he began digging. It was very slow work, because he had to lie on his stomach in the narrow passage and could not dig effectively. He worked on it from time to time without any success. Later, he became too busy with other projects and gave it up. Since that time, other men have tried to connect Buzzards Cave with Crystal Cave through this passage. No one has succeeded.

It will undoubtedly require a lot of dynamiting.

Floyd decided to improve the entrance to Buzzards Cave by building a pathway. There were a number of large rocks, half buried in the ground, that had to be broken up. He carried pick and shovel and a sledge hammer down to the cave and began working on the entrance. Rocks that were too large to move, he broke up with the sledge. There was one big flat rock embedded in the ground in a horizontal position. Floyd cracked it and started to throw the pieces over the bluff. He noticed an odd-looking round object protruding from the dirt beneath the rock. It was a human skull. He laid the sledge aside and carefully picked up the remaining segments of the rock. As he scooped the dirt away, more bones were revealed. He found another skull and the remainder of two skeletons. There were also some beads along with them. He had uncovered a shallow grave by removing the flat rock that had been lying on top of it like a tombstone. Later, Floyd found out that it was an Indian woman and her child buried together at the cave entrance.

Some people say that Floyd found an Indian in Hidden River Cave. According to Floyd, it was not an Indian that he found there, but something of more interest to the police than to archaeologists. Here is how the story got started.

Hidden River Cave is located in the town of Horse Cave fifteen miles from our home. The entrance, a tremendous rock arch, lies beneath the town square. It can be seen from the sidewalk of the main street, a most impressive sight—like looking through a gigantic funnel into the bowels of the earth. Hidden River, a fine source of blind fish, flows through the main gallery of the cave. A few hundred yards down stream from the entrance is Sunset Dome, one of the largest of the underground rooms in the cave region. It is similar to the famous Mountain Room of Wyandotte Cave in both form and size. The ceiling of this dome consists of concentric rings formed as the rocks fell away throughout the ages. Those rocks now form an underground mountain that rises nearly to the ceiling in the center of the dome.

In 1910, Dr. Harry Thomas, owner of Hidden River Cave, hired Floyd to explore it for him. As usual, Floyd undertook the job by himself. He was very enthusiastic about the possibilities of the cave. One morning he found a lantern in a passage. To his surprise it was in good shape. Of course, there had been many people in the cave before him, but why would anyone leave a good lantern behind? He went on. A little later in a muddy passage he came to a ledge about shoulder high. It looked as though there might be a side lead taking off at that point. He noticed a strong odor in the passage. Floyd climbed over the ledge and crawled along, shoving his lantern in front of him. Before he had gone more than a few feet, he found the source of the odor—a human body, badly decomposed. This was no prehistoric man, but a very recent specimen. Judging by his clothing, he had not come in the cave to explore. Floyd crawled over the body to see what was on the other side. The stench was sickening. He could not avoid touching the body. Floyd became very uneasy. For the first time the cave seemed somber, the atmosphere depressing. He decided to call off further exploration. It was necessary to crawl over the body again in order to get out. Floyd shuddered. As he walked toward the entrance, he wanted to look behind—something he knew a lone caver should not do. Once outside the cave, he told Dr. Thomas about finding the body and informed him that he would not go in again. As far as I know, no one ever brought the body out of the cave, and Floyd never returned to find out if it was still there.

Today, anyone who walks down the entrance of Hidden River Cave will encounter the foulest odor that can be imagined. It smells like a thousand bodies rotting inside. Hidden River, which was once pure enough to supply the town of Horse Cave with drinking water, is now a nightmare of pollution. The sewage of the town and surrounding country has been piped into the cave. I suppose you might say it is the world's largest sewer.

Not far from the buzzard's roost, Floyd found an opening in the cliff wall he was afraid to enter. It was a small hole at the bottom of a large rock overhang near the top of the bluff. He wanted to investigate it, but the rocks overhead appeared to be hanging by a hair. He could not get through the opening without disturbing the delicately balanced boulders. One boulder, which measured six feet on a side, seemed to be the keystone holding up all the rest. Floyd became more and more curious. He knew that one false move would bring down an avalanche on top of him, but the situation was intriguing. It was six months before his curiosity finally won out. Early one Sunday morning, he called me aside.

"Skip, do you think you can keep a secret?"

"Sure, Floyd."

"Well, just come on down to the river with me and we'll have a little excitement this morning—if you'll keep quiet about it. Don't let Mamma know where you're going."

Floyd confided in me a great deal. I was always

ready to follow him any time and any place. He knew that I would not let the cat out of the bag for fear that he would no longer take me with him. As we walked toward the bluffs, I kept asking:

"What are you up to, Floyd?"

"Just wait and see," he replied.

I noticed that he was carrying a stick of dynamite. He had been dynamiting for fish earlier in the week, so I figured that this was what he had in mind. However, instead of going to the river, he stopped on the bluff not far from Buzzards Cave.

"What's going on here, Floyd?" I asked.

He pointed to the big overhanging bluff. "Skip, do you see that old bluff there?"

"Yes, what about it?"

"Well, Skip, I'm going to knock that old bluff right over into the river."

"How in the world can you do that?"

"You just get off to the side over there behind one of those big trees and I'll show you."

I ran over to a big tree on the hillside far enough away to be able to watch without being in any danger. Floyd placed the dynamite in a hole in the keystone and very carefully packed it in. He lit the fuse and ran for cover.

"Keep down behind the tree!" he shouted.

I hugged the ground, expecting the entire hillside to disappear. I wanted to watch, but did not dare stick my head out for fear of flying rocks. The charge went off. The explosion was followed by a deep rumble as tons of rock crashed down the hillside, filling the valley with echoes. From a spectator's standpoint, the blast was a complete success. It was as exciting a show as I had ever seen—good clean Sunday fun. However, it did not uncover any cave passage. Floyd was pleased in spite of this, for his curiosity was satisfied at last.

"Well, Skip," he said, "I didn't open any cave for you, but I bet you'll find some mighty fine bow and arrow wood down there among all those splintered hickories."

The boulders smashing against the trees had splintered the trunks. As a boy, I used to make bows and arrows out of hickory, and I placed particular value on trunk wood. Following Floyd's advice, I gathered the splinters from the hickory trunks and made some of my best bows.

Since the authorities frowned on this business of sliding the bluffs into the river channel, Floyd made me promise not to tell anyone. Later we found that the explosion had not gone unnoticed. At Sells Store, the general gathering place in the neighborhood, people were asking if there had been an earthquake down by the river near the Collins place. Floyd and I had a good laugh over the matter and I do not believe anyone ever found out about our Sunday-morning dynamiting party.

Floyd's reputation as a cave explorer began to spread over the countryside. He did not confine his activities to our own ridge, for he was always ready to go exploring no matter where he might be. The country folk thought him curious. He was curious—about the unknown. Today, so many stories are told about his caving feats that it is hard to separate fact from fiction. Old timers will say, "Why I remember one time when Floyd Collins went into a cave over yonder and come up two days later in a field at Cave City ten or fifteen miles away." Or, "Floyd took some dynamite into Salts Cave and twelve hours later we heard blasting miles away over at Ice Cave."

Floyd did not make any elaborate plans for his explorations. Usually his only equipment was a kerosene lantern. He would be thought crude in this era of expeditions—but he got results. He was a one-man expedition. If there was an unexplored hole nearby, Floyd was ready to poke into it just as soon as he could get a lantern. This sometimes led him into difficult situations. For example, there was the time in 1915 when he stopped to explore a pit on his way home from Cave City. The pit had been discovered by Irvin Isenberg, who had a close call doing it. It happened this way.

In the fall of 1914, Lawrence Isenberg was clearing a hillside for planting. The site was about four miles from Cave City near the Shady Grove Church. Irvin, Lawrence's brother, was helping him burn off the grass and leaves. He walked backward across the hillside with a torch in hand, lighting the grass as he went along. Suddenly, his foot plunged through the ground. Almost before he realized what was happening, one leg was in a hole all the way up to the hip. He flattened out on his belly, clutching the solid ground. With his weight spread out, no more ground gave away. He drew his leg out of the hole, then, lying flat on the ground, he dropped his torch into the hole to see what was below. It appeared to be a fairly large pit. As he lay there peering inside, it suddenly occurred to him that he was on turf that might give way at any instant. It covered an area about eight feet in diameter at the top of the pit. Irvin quickly moved away from the hole before any more of the turf collapsed. The hole was left this way all during the winter. Then the spring rains came, causing the rest of the turf to fall in. But no one had the curiosity to go into the pit.

Floyd, walking home from Cave City one day, had stopped to talk with a gang of road workers near the church. Lawrence Isenberg, who was in the crew, told Floyd about the pit and asked if he would like to take a look at it. Floyd said he would go into it just as soon as they could get him a rope and a lantern. Lawrence got a kerosene lantern and the men went to the pit. They placed a stout timber across the top, then tied a piece of rope to the timber. The pit was about sixty feet deep. Floyd went down the rope hand over hand. One man stayed at the top of the pit while the others went back to work.

Floyd was in the pit for about two hours before starting out. He began to pull himself up hand over hand, stopping to rest from time to time by holding onto the rope with a foot lock. However, as he neared the top, his arms began to give out. No matter how long he rested, he could not muster the strength to pull himself up. At the same time, he was becoming too weak to lower himself to the bottom again. To fall would mean sure death. Not enough strength to go up or down—just enough to hold on for a few more seconds.

The man at the top could not help Floyd, for the rope was tied to the timber over the center of the pit. There was no way for him to pull Floyd out, and there was not enough time to run for help.

A few feet away from Floyd, but out of reach, a rock jutted out from the wall. Floyd saw it. He knew that it was his only chance. He must get to that rock fast, and above all, he must not panic. He started the rope swinging back and forth, working in silence. It was only a very short distance, but he was very tired, and there was the problem of letting go of the rope to grab the rock. He put all his energy into one final swing. It carried him all the way to the jutting rock, and he released his grip on the rope. The rope swung back out of reach, and Floyd clung to the rock.

Meanwhile, the man who had stayed with Floyd ran to get the road gang. He told them Floyd was in trouble. They ran to the pit immediately and found Floyd sitting on his perch. Within a few minutes, they had hauled him to the surface. Floyd came out with a big smile on his face—perhaps really a sheepish grin. The men went back to work, and Floyd continued homeward, not stopping by any more caves on the way.

FOUR

Donkey's Cave

During his youth, Floyd worked on the farm, hunted and trapped, cut lumber, sold souvenirs, and in his spare time explored caves. He did any sort of odd job that might be available, for he was handy at nearly everything. Floyd saved his money and kept a bank account in Cave City. He was rather frugal, never spending when he could avoid it, and driving a hard bargain in any transaction. Although very friendly, he would have nothing to do with anyone who tried to get money out of him. He did not make any exceptions with women, having no more inclination to fritter away his money on girls than on anything else that he considered a luxury. Perhaps this accounted for the fact that he was not much interested in women.

Floyd's nearest approach to a love affair came when he was in his teens. At that time the Garvin family lived about a mile from our home. One of the girls, Lulu Garvin, was about the same age as Floyd. She used to come over to our place for eggs, and on these visits she always asked for Floyd. About the only other opportunity they had to get together was at church, for there were no amusement places in that backwoods setting. Sometimes a square dance would be held at a neighbor's house, but there were no dance halls. Nearly everyone in that part of the country was Baptist, and dancing was frowned upon by the stricter members of the church. Floyd attended church regularly, but he was not one of the stricter members.

When Floyd was about twenty-one years old, the Garvins moved out to Oklahoma. Floyd missed Lulu, but he had much work to do, and there was romance in caving.

Floyd felt sure that there were many undiscovered cave passages beneath the ridge around home, but getting into them was not easy. It may seem strange that there should be so many miles of caves in such a small area, and yet so few entrances. Actually there are many small openings, but few that a man can enter. Most of the sinkholes are clogged at the bottom with debris that has washed in. The ridge-tops are covered with a thick protective layer of sandstone, which, more resistant than limestone, hinders the development of openings at the top of the ridge. Entrances are found for the most part down in the valleys. As the valleys were cut deeper over a long period of time, the cave passages underlying the ridges were exposed. It is possible to find these entrances as you walk along the surface, even though they are partially hidden by the rock and earth that has crept down the hillside over the centuries.

Floyd searched the woods for cave openings. On cold winter mornings, he used to look for clouds of steam rising out of the ground. These steam clouds are formed by condensation of water vapor when the relatively warm air from underground comes in direct contact with the colder air outside. Floyd found many blow-holes in this manner, but few that he could get into without digging. Usually, the hole was just a vent that nothing but a small animal could get through. In the most remote cave passages Floyd often found animal tracks, nuts, twigs, and leaves where one of these small vents provided an entrance for pack rats.

Floyd found several caves near home on a tract of land owned by the Louisville and Nashville Railroad. They contained some nice onyx formations, but as Floyd could not obtain a lease on the land, he just forgot where the entrances were located. In fact, he did such a good job forgetting them that they are still forgotten today.

By the time Floyd reached manhood, he had saved enough money to buy land for farming. He bought sixty acres from George Kline in the valley west of our home. The hillside was rather steep for plowing, but Floyd had as much patience as his old mule, Kate, and was equally stubborn. One day he was plowing the steep slope near the bottom of the valley when suddenly Kate fell to her knees. He tried to get her started again, but she wouldn't budge. When Floyd looked to see what was wrong he found one leg caught in a hole. After getting Kate out of her predicament, he removed the sod from around the hole, and then he dug away enough to reveal a sizable pit. There was not enough light to see what it was like at the bottom, but as he lay there peering into the hole he could feel the cold air pouring out. Surely this was a cave, perhaps a big one, on his own farm. And it was only a few hundred yards from

Pike Chapman's Entrance to Great Salts Cave. There might be a connection between them.

    The plowing was forgotten. Floyd went to the cabin for rope to get into the pit. He tied it to a stout pole that he laid across the opening. Because of the steepness of the slope at that point, he found it necessary to drive stakes into the ground to hold the pole in place. There was still a lot of loose material around the edge of the hole. Floyd was very anxious to get into the pit, but he remembered the Pike Chapman incident. First he had to make sure that there was no danger of anything falling in on him, for he knew that even a small rock could be as deadly as a bullet if it fell any distance. He cleared away the loose material, and after a final check for head busters, let himself down hand-over-hand on the rope. In a few seconds he was standing at the bottom of the pit, or rather on a pile of rock and mud that filled the bottom. If there was any way on, it was blocked by this debris that had fallen in, but Floyd was heartened by the cold air that poured out from under the rocks at his feet. Convinced that there was passage not far below, he began digging into the muck with his bare hands. He hoped that he could open a hole large enough to squeeze through for a preliminary look, but it was impossible. The pit was only three feet wide at the bottom, so there was no place to pile the material that he dug out. Floyd was covered with mud from head to foot and was sweating in the damp cold. His hands were sore. Finally, he climbed out of the pit and went to ask Andy Lee to help him haul the material out of the pit. Andy Lee agreed to help, so they went to the pit equipped with a bucket and pulley for lifting the material to the surface. While Floyd stayed at the bottom to dig and fill the bucket, Andy Lee manned the rope at the top, dumping the material out on the hillside. The work proceeded very slowly, for there was not much room to maneuver at the bottom. The shaft was too narrow to swing a pick in. Floyd had to pick up the rocks he stood on—somewhat like pulling the rug out from under his own feet. Digging was also very difficult because of the mud. Even the rock walls were wet and slimy, and water dripped down constantly. Fortunately there was not enough water to create a stream, just enough to make it unpleasantly muddy. Floyd worked in this muck for several hours.

The shaft narrowed as it deepened, so work became progressively more difficult. However, the draft of air coming up kept Floyd's hopes high. Finally, he made an opening barely large enough to squeeze through. He squirmed through the hole, slid down a few feet, and found himself in the cave at last. After shouting to Andy Lee that he had broken into horizontal passage, Floyd turned up his lantern and examined the cave. He found a fine display of grape formation. This peculiar form of onyx grows from the rock in clusters that look for all the world like bunches of grapes. Farther on, Floyd found a canyon-shaped side passage leading to a stream. He continued down the main passage for a couple of hundred yards and found some stalagmites and stalactites. Upon tapping the stalactites, he found that they gave a musical ring, each of a slightly different pitch. In his excitement, he had nearly forgotten about Andy Lee waiting outside, but he thought he had better return before Andy Lee became worried about his absence. At the entrance, Floyd began to describe the cave breathlessly as he climbed out of the pit.

"Andy, this may be worth more than the whole farm. I believe it would make a fine show cave if only we could make a good entrance and get the people over here."

"What did you find inside, Floyd?"

"Very fine grape formations and nice onyx. It looks pretty good."

Floyd climbed out on the surface and discussed with Andy Lee the possibilities of opening the cave to the public. A great deal of loose rock and mud would have to be cleared out of the pit before the horizontal passage could be entered without sliding in like a snake. Floyd diverted water into the entrance to wash out the muck from the bottom of the pit. This was much easier than digging it out, and it did not keep him from his other work. Later, he built a small house directly over the entrance to keep the rain water out of the cave. A stout wooden ladder afforded access from this house to the passage below.

Mr. Wade Highbaugh, a photographer at Mammoth Cave, came over to photograph the cave for Floyd. Floyd experimented with the musical stalactites until he was able to play tunes by tapping on them. After awhile he became pretty good at this highly specialized art of underground music, and he often stopped to practice on his onyx xylophone. The tune he played best was his favorite hymn, "Nearer My God to Thee." When Mother died in 1915, he had this same hymn sung over her grave at the funeral.

Because of the accident that resulted in the discovery of the cave, Floyd named it Donkey's Cave. He decided it would be better to have a horizontal entrance rather than a vertical shaft, so he began work on a tunnel farther down the hillside at the same level as the cave passage. However, he never got around to completing this entrance. Floyd kept fodder in the house over the top of the pit. This was a cool place owing to the continual draft of air from the cave, which stayed at a constant temperature the year around.

Floyd used to keep apples in with the fodder, and one day we went down to the cave together to bring a few apples up to the house. Floyd was wearing a clean white shirt and took great pains to see that it remained spotless. It was a warm day, so he had the collar unbuttoned. While we were inside the house, a lizard dropped on Floyd and found its way beneath his shirt through the open collar. As the lizard explored its new surroundings, Floyd jumped and let out a yell. "There's something down my back, Skip. Grab it!"

I reached down inside Floyd's shirt and caught the lizard by the tail. It felt like a snake to me, but I held on anyway. The tail broke off in my hand. "It's a snake!" I yelled, throwing the lizard's tail to the ground.

Floyd nearly tore the shirt off his back. Both of us had a good laugh when we found out that it was only a harmless lizard. Floyd's shirt was a mess by this time and he looked at it rather sadly. Then he laughed and turned to me. "Well, Skip, what do you say we take a few apples and get back to the house?"

The pit leading into Donkey's Cave was partially filled some years ago, and in the winter of 1954 a group of about ten young men armed with picks, shovels, rope, buckets, and other equipment decided to open it again. They used the same method Floyd and Andy Lee had used many years before, but with less success. All but two of the group gave up after one trip to the bottom, saying that it was too dangerous. Those two finally concluded that it was too much work for them alone. The project was abandoned, with due respect to the explorer who seldom allowed any such obstacle to defeat him. The cave was later reopened after a dozen or so young men worked at the project for several weeks.

FIVE

Edmund Turner

Edmund Turner, the man to whom Floyd had sold moccasins, returned to the cave region in 1910. Turner, a geologist, came to study terrain and rock formation, but he was also interested in caves as an explorer. At Mammoth Cave he had asked one of the guides, "Do you know any good explorers in the neighborhood?"

"Yes," he said, "the Collins boy is about the best around here. He just discovered a cave on his own farm."

"I met a boy when I was down here several years ago, *Floyd* Collins."

"That's him."

"So he's found a cave now. How can I get in touch with him?"

The guide told him how to get to the farm, and Turner set out to pay Floyd a visit. Old man Bivin Houchins brought Turner over in a horse-drawn wagon, the nearest thing to a taxi service in the region. Floyd was delighted to meet Turner once again, and they immediately began talking caves. Within a few minutes they were lost in the underground world, unaware of the rest of the family around them. The conversation continued for several hours. Floyd invited Turner to stay overnight, promising to show him Donkey's Cave next day. The next morning, they went to the cave and spent the day together. When they returned to the house, Mother was preparing supper. "Mrs. Collins," Turner said, "I'd like to board here with you folks for a while."

Mother was surprised. "You're from the big city," she said. "Why in the world do you want to stay here?"

"I came down here to study geology and I'm interested in caves. This is a perfect location. Besides, Floyd can be of great help to me. We get along very well."

Mother had taken an immediate liking to Turner. "Well, we're kind of crowded, but we'll put you up."

She charged him $2.50 a week for room and board. This may seem rather cheap, but a dollar was a dollar at that time, and besides, we raised most of our own food. Most important of all, he was a very likable person and extremely interesting. It was a pleasure to have him around. Turner had a room all to himself, an annex that had been built onto the house. Between his room and the rest of the house there was a little hallway. This served as a bedroom for Floyd, Andy Lee, Marshall, and me.

Turner did a great deal of writing, and he used to send me over to Sells Store after tablets. He would give me a dollar and tell me to keep the change, so I made a special point of being available for running errands. He always insisted on complete privacy when writing, but he was not the least bit aloof. As a matter of fact, in spite of his education and different background, he adjusted to our way of life easily. It was as though he had been raised in the Kentucky hills rather than New York. He was quiet, well mannered, and friendly. Oftentimes we would sit on the ground on summer evenings listening to him telling stories that he had made up. One story concerned a man discovering a cave. History has it that Mammoth Cave was discovered by a hunter who was chasing a bear. Turner used a slightly different twist, having the man discover the cave with the bear hot at his heels.

Floyd showed Turner the countryside and took him through numerous caves. After seeing Great Salts Cave, Turner caught the same fever that gripped Floyd. The scientific man was becoming a confirmed cave addict. He offered to pay Floyd two dollars a day to explore with him. Floyd accepted the offer, for it was not all that uncommon around home to put in a hard day's labor for seventy-five cents, and here was an opportunity to go caving—his favorite pastime—for high wages. So began the most unique partnership in the history of the cave region, the scientific and the practical man working together, each learning from the other. Floyd was twenty-three, Turner was about forty. Both men were loners, capable of carrying on by themselves if the need arose. In this age of expeditions with the stress on teamwork, this quality is sometimes overlooked, but it was men such as Floyd Collins and Edmund Turner who made possible the expeditions that were to follow.

Edmund Turner was convinced from his study of the geology of Flint Ridge that it contained an enormous system of caverns, even greater in extent than Mammoth Cave. He felt that Great Salts Cave was the key to this system. But the big problem was to get from the known passages into the undiscovered portion. From theoretical considerations the passages had to be there—finding them was a tough job.

Floyd and Turner started working in Great Salts Cave. They explored and surveyed, sometimes

Edmund Turner.
Mammoth Cave National Park Collection.

staying underground for days at a time. Often they would bring out Indian relics, which Turner packed in boxes and sent away. As the weeks passed, they became more and more enthusiastic about their work. Turner was apparently well satisfied with the results. At first they talked freely about their explorations, showing us maps Turner had made of the passages they had surveyed. But then a change occurred. No longer did Turner permit us to see his maps. His survey notes were kept under lock. When they talked about their work, the conversation became guarded. From that time forward, everything was secret.

Ordinarily when men make a discovery, they are eager to let the world know about it. Why the secrecy? Floyd and Turner had undoubtedly discovered something worthwhile. This was evident from their actions and enthusiasm. It seemed that they should have been proud to show their discoveries to other people. But cavers such as Floyd and Edmund Turner are not ordinary people. A cave explorer goes through unbelievably difficult places, risking his life to reach some remote passage where no man has set foot before. And once in a lifetime, with luck, he makes a truly outstanding discovery. Perhaps it is a rare and beautiful formation. The remoteness adds to its beauty. It has never been seen by any human being; maybe no one should ever see it after him. He thinks of the commercialized caves, the crowds of tourists laughing, dropping candy wrappers and cigarette butts, looking for every opportunity to pick up a souvenir or scratch initials on the rocks. Is it worthwhile? Are people so important? There below ground, hidden and silent, hallowed by the absence of man, somehow things seem right as they are.

During the time that Turner stayed at our house, he worked six days a week, exploring, surveying, mapping, writing, and doing odd jobs like any country handyman. But Sunday was his day of rest. I don't believe he ever worked on Sunday while he lived with us. However, in spite of this self-imposed rule, he did not attend church. One Sunday morning my father asked him if he would care to go along with us to church. Turner politely declined the invitation.

"Have you ever thought about the hereafter?" Pap said. "Have you ever thought about Hell?"

"No, I haven't given that much thought. You know, a man usually finds what he looks for. I'm not looking for those places." The subject was never mentioned again.

Floyd, on the other hand, attended church regularly. Floyd and my sister Annie were baptized in the year 1911 where the Mammoth Cave Ferry crossed the Green River. But Floyd felt that religion consisted of something more than mere church attendance. The work of God was more evident to him in the barren rocks of a cave passage than in the little wooden building where many came to profess their religion and few left to practice it.

Our preacher, a man by the name of Shepherd, had rather peculiar ways. Preacher Shep, as we called him, used to visit different homes in the neighborhood, and on one occasion he stopped at our house for dinner. Mother prepared a sumptuous meal: fried chicken, vegetables, rolls, her best preserves, everything. Preacher Shep sat down and we bowed our heads as he gave thanks to the Lord for our many blessings. When the prayer was over he surveyed the heaping table. Then, breaking off a piece of cornbread, he asked for a glass of buttermilk. "I'm very fond of cornbread and buttermilk," he said.

Mother brought him some buttermilk, and he made a meal of the cornbread and buttermilk while the rest of us, feeling like gluttons, filled ourselves with the delicious meal that had been prepared for him.

Floyd learned a great deal about geology from Edmund Turner. Turner explained to him that the limestone was formed from deposits that had been laid down at the bottom of a sea that had covered a large part of the United States millions of years ago. This accounted for the presence of marine fossils embedded in the rock. After the sea had retreated, the rainwater began its work of carving out passages, finding its way through the joints and crevices in the rocks as it flowed beneath the surface. The valleys cut into the flanks of the ridge, exposing the long-hidden cave passages in the process. The upper levels of the caves were left high and dry as the Green River cut its way deeper and deeper. Meanwhile, numerous sink holes were formed, giving the region its peculiar surface pattern. And this process was still going on beneath their very feet.

Turner lived with us for two years, and we considered him as one of the family. But Mother was suffering from tuberculosis, and Turner, feeling that he was creating an extra burden on her, moved away. He did not leave the cave region, for he had been completely overcome, just as Floyd had, by the lure of the underground world. He and Floyd still did some work together.

Floyd sought any information that he could find on the subject of geology. Colonel Lucien Beckner, a well-known consulting geologist who now resides in Louisville and is in charge of the natural history museum there, formerly did some work in the cave region. Many times he sat on the doorstep of the house talking with Floyd. He says Floyd had a very inquiring mind, and that it was impossible for a geologist to go anywhere near the Collins' farm without being collared by the questioning explorer.

Several miles down the Green River near the Mammoth Cave Ferry there was a general store run by Lenny Dossey. On the hillside not far from the store a draft of air came out of a small opening. Edmund Turner dug into it, and with Floyd discovered a cave. The cave, a series of domes with onyx formations, was exhibited to the public for a time under the name of Dossey's Dome Cave.

In 1915, Turner went to work for L. P. Edwards, a former preacher at the Mammoth Cave Church. Preacher Edwards had a river-bottom farm on the Green River two miles from our home. Turner had surveyed parts of Great Salts Cave that extended beneath Edwards' property. He had seen an outcrop of onyx on the hillside and limestone boulders standing on end instead of lying in the normal position. To Turner's experienced eye, this was an exposed cave passage, a collapsed cavern nearly hidden by debris from the hillside.

According to Turner, Preacher Edwards had promised him half-interest in the cave, if he found one. Turner began digging, and soon the cave was opened. It was commercialized, and they called it Great Onyx Cave. When Turner asked for his half-interest, Edwards denied that he had made such an agreement. Turner sued, but there was no written contract, and he lost the suit. He became depressed.

Exploration had been elating; the business world was hard. He returned to Great Salts Cave and sealed the connection between it and Great Onyx.

"There are five miles of cave," Turner said, "that Preacher Edwards will never see." These five miles were not seen by Preacher Edwards, nor have they been rediscovered up to this day.

Turner knew that Great Onyx Cave crossed under the boundary line of Edwards' farm, so he decided to try digging an entrance on a neighboring farm. Regardless of where the natural entrance to a cave is located or where an entrance is first discovered, each part belongs to the owner of the land directly above. The property lines extend straight down indefinitely. Pate Lee had a farm adjoining Preacher Edwards' property, and Turner was staying at Pate Lee's home after his trouble with Edwards. The survey showed that much of Great Onyx Cave ran under Lee's property. Turner also knew that part of it ran under the Frank Davis farm, and he figured that there would be a good possibility of getting into the cave on Davis' place. He began working there in an attempt to dig a new entrance.

During the same year that Great Onyx Cave was discovered, Floyd moved into an old log cabin on his farm. Andy Lee and his wife lived there with Floyd and helped him work on the farm. Mother's condition became so bad after spring planting that Floyd moved back home to stay with her. She died that summer.

Meanwhile, Edmund Turner was suffering from a stomach ailment. His condition became steadily worse, until he could no longer work. Finally, he was taken in by a relative of Pate Lee, one-eyed Joe Lee, who lived by himself down on the Green River below Mammoth Cave. Turner was in a helpless condition. With no income, he could not afford medical care. The man who brought about a new era of exploration in the cave region was only a shadow. There was nothing left to him but his memories. He died in the year 1919. We felt as if one of our own family had passed away. Floyd remarked, "The cave region has lost its greatest explorer." Edmund Turner was buried in an unmarked grave in the cemetery of Mammoth Cave Church near the grave of my mother. The knowledge of many caverns was buried with him, caverns that have yet to be rediscovered.

Among the papers that Turner left behind were his survey notes for Great Onyx Cave. Pate Lee knew from these notes that part of the cave ran under his property. In 1928, he brought suit against L. P. Edwards, who had been showing part of the cave that actually belonged to him. It was proven that part of route number one and all of route number two ran under Lee's property, but he had not received any compensation. Pate Lee won the suit, and in 1936 the Court of Appeals upheld a decision awarding approximately twenty-five thousand dollars to the estate of Pate Lee as its share of the net profit derived from the operation of Great Onyx Cave during the years 1925 through 1930. About one-third of the cave ran under their land, so the estate was given one third of the profits.

The last time I saw Preacher Edwards, he was in Horse Cave trying to borrow some money. I had just returned from a tour on the Pantages Theatre circuit, and he asked me if I could lend him any money. I had other plans at the time.

"Pate Lee nearly wrecked me with that suit," he said. I did not answer him, for I could only think of

Edmund Turner who had died penniless. Edmund Turner's passing marked the close of a most important chapter in Floyd's life, for Floyd was enormously influenced by this extraordinary man.

SIX

The Great Discovery

When Edmund Turner moved out of our house, he left a number of geology books for Floyd. Floyd read through them, and he knew as much about the geology of caves as was known at that time. His curiosity more than made up for his lack in formal education. Turner had shown him that what seemed to be a maze of caverns without order was actually a system. It was a labyrinth that existed on several levels, complicated by the many breakdowns between levels, mud, and endless winding crawlways. Floyd was fascinated by the geological study of the caves, but he was an explorer first. Even with a thorough knowledge of the geological setup, an explorer must poke into every hole, squirm through every crevice, climb the walls, move rocks, and swim to find the cave he suspects is there.

Caving was a hobby to Floyd. Sometimes he was paid to investigate a cave, but there was not enough money in it for a full-time job. He made his living on his farm, in the woods, by hunting and trapping, and by doing odd jobs. There was virgin timber around home, and each year we cut some of it for the mill. The Green River offered a ready means of transportation to the lumber mill. Each year we got together about a thousand logs and rafted them downstream.

In the fall, we began cutting the big trees into logs. When the ground was frozen hard in the wintertime, we snaked logs into the chute leading down to the river. Old Sam and Buck, a pair of oxen, pulled the logs to the chute. Four of us worked at the riverbank rafting the logs. Two men put the logs under the raft, one man bored holes for the wooden pegs that held the logs in place, and one man drove the pegs through the support into the logs. The logs had to be held together by wooden pegs, as the lumber mill would not accept any with nails in them. After working all day, Floyd used to sit up past midnight whittling pegs with a two-handed draw knife.

When the raft was completed, we built a small hut on top of it and placed a stove inside. The hut was kitchen, office, and warming spot on the long journey downstream. Ordinarily, the river was not high enough to take a big raft to the mill, so we had to wait until the water was up. Rafting was made difficult by the narrowness of the Green River and its sharp bends and islands. At high water, the stream was very swift. The mill was located at Evansville, Indiana, a distance of well over a hundred miles. Usually about eight or ten men went along, and it took them about three weeks to reach their destination.

I accompanied Floyd on some trips when I was in my early teens. Once when I was very young, I sneaked aboard and hid in the shack until they were under way. When my brothers discovered me, it was too late to send me back, so they let me make the trip. However, I had to stay in the shack most of the time and cook for them.

As a boy Floyd saved Pap's life while taking a raft of logs down the river. Pap had fallen off the raft and was being carried away by the current. The temperature was near freezing, and he could not swim with his boots and heavy clothing dragging him down. Floyd heard Pap shout and saw him struggling against the current. He grabbed one of the long poles used for hooking logs and hooked Pap around the body. Pap was nearly frozen when Floyd pulled him aboard, but he thawed out by the fire in a few minutes.

Logging was hard work, sometimes dangerous, but always interesting. After delivering the logs to the mill, Floyd would walk back home along the banks of the river. On those journeys, he would often stop to investigate any openings that looked like cave entrances. I was smaller than he at the time, and so it frequently fell my lot to wiggle into the tighter holes.

One day in September 1917, Floyd and I went down to the river to mark some trees we planned to cut for the winter's logging operation. After selecting the trees, we started back up the hill. It was a long climb to the top of the bluff, and the day was exceptionally warm. We had worked up quite a sweat and were looking for a shady place to rest before returning to the house. Near the top of the hill, there were two big sandstone boulders, each as large as a room of a house, leaning against each other, forming a shelter between them. We stopped and sat in the shade beneath the rocks. As we rested there, Floyd noticed a draft of cold air coming out of a small hole in the ground. He got on his knees and scratched the dirt away until he could see into the hole. It appeared to open below into a larger space. The hole was too small for either of us to get through. "I believe we've got a cave here," he said. "You run on up to the house and bring back a pick and shovel. Better get a crowbar, too, and a lantern."

While I went after the tools, he began digging with his hands. When I returned, Floyd had already enlarged the hole quite a bit. He used the crowbar to pry loose a few stones, and it was big enough to enter with ease. He went inside and dropped down about ten feet to the bottom. He was in a small cavity that seemed to be part of a passage, but there were a lot of loose rocks in the way. Floyd's curiosity would not let him stop there. He began moving rocks. There was no place to dispose of the rocks except out on the surface, so he relayed them up to me by hand. Finally he broke into the passage. There was a pit in the floor just inside the passage, and a narrow ledge crossed over the top of it along the right-hand wall. By scooting across this ledge he was able to get to the other side without climbing down into the pit. He walked about a hundred feet farther to a wall of breakdown that closed off the passage. These breakdowns, which are huge piles of loose rock, very often seal off passages. Sometimes they are so large that they form underground mountains, one of the most awesome sights in a cave. The breakdown that stopped Floyd was not so large, but it completely filled the passage. He saw that it would require much rock moving to go any farther, and decided to leave it for another day. However, he noticed that this little segment of cave would make a good storage cellar. Later on he carried a bushel of apples to the cave, leaving them there to keep for Christmas. That was in the month of September. For the next few months, the cave was forgotten as Floyd had lots of work to keep him busy.

On December 17, 1917, Floyd took a notion to go down to the cave for some of the apples that he had left there. A heavy snow had fallen, so he took a shovel with him to clear the entrance. He left the house without telling anyone where he was going. At the entrance he removed all the loose material from around the hole before going into the pit. Inside, the air was much warmer, although a strong draft blew through the passage. He found the bushel of apples, or what was left of them, badly mutilated. Pack rats had carried off most of the apples, leaving only a few scraps. These pack rats, also called wood rats, are found in nearly all the caves. They are native to this country, unlike the house rat, which was introduced from abroad. They are not the same as the familiar garbage rooters that inhabit every city, lurking in basements and alleys. Pack rats are friendly little critters by comparison. They can easily be distinguished from their offensive city cousins by the fact that their ears and tails are covered with hair. The Norwegian rat has no hair on its ears and tail. The name pack rat was given to them because of their habit of packing home useless objects. They are natural thieves. It must be said in their defense, however, that they often leave a stick or a stone in place of the stolen article. I have known them to carry off flash bulbs stashed in a cave passage by an unwary photographer.

Floyd noticed a trail of scraps leading away from the bushel of apples. He followed the trail to the end of the passage, where the breakdown had halted him three months before. The rats had been dragging their loot away through the pile of loose rock. Perhaps there was big cave beyond; the draft of air was strong enough. The rats had gone through the breakdown, and Floyd decided he would try to go through. It was not possible for him to squeeze through without moving the rocks. Floyd began pulling them out, gradually working his way through. It was ticklish business. In places he found a crevice that he could snake through, but most of the time he had to make his own crevices. He had to know which rocks could be safely moved and which ones might cause a slide.

There was no way of knowing whether this passage was blocked for only a few feet or for many yards. Hours passed, and Floyd was still faced with more loose rocks. The current of air coming through the breakdown kept him from becoming discouraged. He had advanced only a few yards, for it was very difficult to get the rocks out of the way once he was inside the breakdown. There was barely room enough to slide his body through.

Imagine yourself suspended in a matrix of broken rocks, not knowing when they might slide. You lie there with the jagged edges digging into your body, and try to move a rock from in front of you, so that you can inch forward. You have no leverage and no room to work. Your body takes up nearly all the space, so there is hardly any place to put the rocks after dislodging them. Floyd worked under these conditions all day before he finally broke through into open passage. It was a relief to stand again after lying on sharp edged rocks all day.

Within a few feet Floyd came to a steep slope. The ceiling, which was so flat it looked like it had been plastered, continued at the same level. The floor dropped far below—how far he could not tell. He held his lantern up for a better view, but the gallery before him was too large to be seen by its light. It was like standing at the edge of a cliff on the blackest night, peering into space. Slowly he made his way down the hill, stepping cautiously on the boulders as he went along. He was in a great underground canyon, larger than any he had ever seen or heard of. The walls had been sculptured by water into long, graceful curves. No artist could have done better. At the bottom of the canyon, Floyd found another large passage intersecting it at right angles. Straight ahead, the floor of the canyon sloped up again and disappeared into the darkness. Floyd stood motionless for a long time, awed by the cavern that had lain hidden beneath his very home. He wanted to shout, to sing, to talk to someone. He stood there alone, silent. This moment made his years of exploration worthwhile. It was his own underground world, bounded by stone walls and darkness.

But there was more cave to be explored. He took the right-hand branch of the cross-passage leading out from the bottom of the canyon. Within a few feet he made another discovery, a petrified flower garden growing from the ceiling and sparkling like a bed of diamonds. Every inch of the wall and ceiling for about thirty feet was covered with crystalline flowers. They were formed from gypsum, a mineral that produces fibrous growths that resemble roses, lilies, and strange flowers never before seen. The color varies from pure white to orange and brown. It is, perhaps, the most beautiful of all cave formations.

In a cranny on the opposite side of the passage,

Floyd found a deposit of Epsom salts. It was the same snowy-white formation that he had seen in Great Salts Cave. Farther on he found another type of gypsum. The wall appeared to be covered with a thick coat of sparkling brown sugar. He pushed on, at every step noticing holes that might lead to other passages. Finally he came to a breakdown that blocked the passage. There seemed to be a way of crawling around it along the right-hand wall. Then Floyd thought about his light; it was nearly out of oil. No one knew where he was. In his enthusiasm he had lost track of time. He turned around at once and began retracing his steps toward the entrance. He did not stop to admire the formations. If his light gave out, it might be a long time before anyone found him. Reentering the canyon was like walking out of the cave into the outdoors. He scrambled over the

Gypsum flowers. *Photo by Russell T. Neville. CRF Collection.*

The Collins home on Flint Ridge, just one hundred yards from where Floyd discovered Crystal Cave.
Photo by Russell T. Neville. CRF Collection.

rocks up the steep canyon hill and went on to the breakdown. Tired, he did not stop to rest, for he could not pick his way through the breakdown without light. From the other side, even if the lantern were to go out, he could probably feel his way to the entrance. He began to thread his way between the rocks, shoving the lantern in front of him, carefully avoiding the loose rocks that a hasty move could dislodge. In five minutes he squirmed through the tortuous path that had required hours to open. The light held out, and he reached the entrance without incident.

It was dark outside when Floyd climbed out of the pit. He was covered with sweat and grime. His body steamed as he stood in the cold air, resting for a few seconds under the boulders that sheltered the entrance. Then he hurried up the hill to the house. We were all in bed when he came pounding on the door. Ordinarily Floyd was calm and quiet. We knew there was something mighty unusual to make him excited. He spoke breathlessly. "I discovered a cave—the biggest I've ever seen. It's full of gypsum flowers and crystals. Look at this." He showed me a piece of gypsum that he had picked up from the floor of the cave.

"It's the little cave down the hill where I had the apples stored. I ran out of oil and had to come out, but there's lots more exploring to do. I'll get some sleep, and then we'll go down there first thing in the morning."

When daylight broke on the eighteenth, I went to a neighbor's house to borrow oil for the lantern as our own supply was low. The exploring party consisted of Floyd, Marshall, and me. Pap warned us to be careful as we filled our lanterns and left the house. At the cave, Floyd took the lead. We followed him through the breakdown and on to the canyon. Even though he had described it to us, we were amazed. I had been in many large caverns, but none like this. There is a sweep to the walls that makes it more impressive than the size alone—sheer walls that rise to a flat ceiling that extends all the way back to the entrance on the same level. Floyd decided to call it the Grand Canyon.

At the bottom of the canyon we went out the side passage to the left, which ended in a big, wet breakdown. There were some pits here, too. We decided to leave them for another day and explore the passage where Floyd had turned around the night before. Wet breakdowns are extremely treacherous. The one where Floyd had turned around was dry, so we headed for it. At the breakdown Floyd crawled over the rocks, keeping to the right hand wall. There was just enough space for us to slide through. Floyd led

Floyd's Grand Canyon.
Photo by Roger E. McClure.

the way, moving rocks where necessary, and in a few minutes we were through the breakdown. The passage went on. It was big and rugged, like the main passage of Great Salts Cave.

We pushed on as rapidly as the hills and valleys and boulders in the passage would permit. Then we came to one of the wildest-looking rooms I have ever seen. There was a big slump in the floor, a breakdown on the far side, and huge slabs of limestone littering the room. We named it the Devil's Kitchen. A side passage skirted the breakdown to the right. The main passage veered sharply to the left, seeming to double back on itself. This was undoubtedly the intersection of two big passages. We turned left and found a pit and dome at the bend in the passage. Water dripped out of the dome above and formed a clear pool in the pit below. Today, the visitors to Crystal Cave stop here for a drink. We called it the Dripping Spring. The passage had been dry up to that point, and the spring gave us a source of drinking water for exploring farther in that section of cave.

Beyond the spring we came to a steep slope that was very slippery. We slid down this slope and went on to dry passage once more. Floyd later called this slippery valley the Wine Cellar. "They whine going down, and they whine coming up." Today the Wine Cellar is still there, but the whine is gone.

Beyond the Wine Cellar, we found a great concentration of crystal formation. The walls of the passage were completely covered with sparkling gypsum of every description. Even the rocks on the floor were crusted with it, and we could not take a step without treading on it. Long, thin crystals lay scattered about like splinters of glass. Crystal flowers

The Collins family. *Photo from Howard W. Hartley's* Tragedy of Sand Cave.

sparkled in the lights of our lanterns—the first light that had ever fallen on them.

After walking about a quarter of a mile, we came to a huge boulder wedged between the walls of the passage. We ducked under the boulder and noted a crawlway that intersected the main passage at that point. The duck-under, later called Scotchman's Trap, was to become famous among cavers as a starting point for adventure. We continued at a fast pace, without stopping to investigate any crawlways. Finally we came to a breakdown that blocked the passage. The presence of sandstone indicated it was close to the surface. Floyd looked it over. "We won't fool with it," he said. "Let's head back now and tell Pap what we found."

SEVEN

GREAT CRYSTAL CAVE

We decided at once to commercialize the cave. Since it ran under Pap's land, the cave belonged to him, but he deeded Floyd a half interest. It was first called Great Gypsum Cave. Later, the name was changed to Great Crystal Cave, and now, of course, it is called Floyd Collins Crystal Cave.

To make the cave a tourist attraction required much work. Tourists don't like to get dirty; they don't want to skip from rock to rock, climb over boulders, or crawl on their bellies. We had to enlarge the entrance and make tunnels through the two breakdowns. There had to be an easy walking, thoroughly safe path. We wanted to have the cave ready for the summer of 1918, and it was already late December, 1917. Pap sold some cattle to hire outside help, and we began work immediately.

The pit just inside the entrance presented quite a problem. Floyd decided to blast the roof of the entrance in, then use the material to fill the pit to make a level walkway. The blasting would close the entrance temporarily, but Floyd thought it would be easier to dig it open again with someone helping from the inside. No one but Floyd would volunteer to go below, so he went in by himself. He took plenty of food and light with him in case we should run into any trouble. He went far back into the passage and waited for us to dynamite. On the surface there were, besides me, Pap, Andy Lee, Marshall, and Bob

Homer Collins (left) and his brother Andrew at the Cyrstal Cave office. *Photo from Howard W. Hartley's* Tragedy of Sand Cave.

Adwell. When the blasting was finished, the two boulders that sheltered the entrance were blown into small fragments, and the entrance was completely closed.

At first we could not communicate with Floyd. We began digging as fast as possible. Within an hour there was a deep hole that slowed us down somewhat since the rocks had to be lifted out. The deeper the hole became, the more work it was to relay the rocks and dirt outside. Still we could not hear Floyd. In spite of our confidence in him, we felt uneasy, for it appeared that the work would require considerable time. After about two hours, we heard a clicking sound from below. Floyd was okay. We couldn't talk to him yet. We knew his voice would not carry more than a few feet through the rock and dirt. Signaling in a cave is always done by pounding on rocks, even in open passage. It is surprising how well this sound carries through the rock, but a voice is lost around a few bends in the passage.

Inside the cave, Floyd was not spending all his time trying to signal us. He dumped load after load of rock into the pit, determined not to stop until the entrance was open. You or I, in the same circumstances, would probably be overcome with fear of being trapped, but he had spent so much time below ground that these things didn't bother him. He had figured it would take quite a few hours. Once inside, his thoughts were concentrated on the work. This was neither the time nor the place to worry.

It took thirty hours to dig through. Floyd was in excellent spirits when we reached him, but had no objection to knocking off work for the day.

Later, we cleaned out all the loose rock, built a stone stairway into the cave, and filled the pit completely, making the floor level at the entrance. Then, we made a tunnel through the two breakdowns that blocked the passages. Tourists can recognize these tunnels easily, for they are the only narrow places in the passage. Beyond the Dripping Spring, we filled in the bottom of the Wine Cellar, leaving only a slight dip in the floor. All winter we worked on the trails, breaking up boulders and hauling dirt from one part of the cave to lay on the path in another.

We had neither the time nor the money to install an adequate lighting system before the start of the tourist season, so we decided to use lanterns. This presented a problem in the Grand Canyon, for the room was too big to be seen that way. To throw more light on the canyon, we built a hoist so that a lantern could be raised high above the floor. It was not until after the expedition in 1954 that an adequate system of electric lights was installed. Bill Austin and Jim Dyer crawled out on a narrow ledge at the top of the canyon to install indirect lighting. Now the flat ceiling looks like a river of light.

One day in the spring of 1918, Floyd was gone from the house all day. No one had seen him outside, and he had not told anyone where he was going. Toward evening, I felt uneasy about his absence and decided to look for him. He often worked in the cave by himself, so I got a lantern and started down the hill. At the entrance I found Floyd's dog Obie on guard. Obie, a chow, had been given to me by my brother Jim in 1915, shortly after Mother died. The dog paid no attention to me. However, he took a liking to Floyd and followed him everywhere he went—except into a cave. Whenever Floyd went into a cave, Obie waited at the entrance until he came out. If Floyd left any article outside, Obie would not let anyone touch it, no matter how well he knew them. He was a one-man dog.

We had named the dog Obie in memory of another dog of ours that had died some years before. When Floyd was just a boy, Pap had a dog named Rover. Floyd, who was just a toddler at the time we got the dog, could not pronounce the word Rover correctly. When he tried to say Rover it always came out Obie instead. Years later, Rover met his death in the cold waters of Pike Spring one day while Floyd was hunting along the river bluffs. The dog was running down the steep hillside, and when he reached the ledge over the top of the spring he was not able to check his momentum. He plunged over the ledge and into the spring. The water was very deep and it flowed rapidly into the Green River, which was only a few yards away. Floyd shouted to Rover, but he received no answer. Climbing down the hill to the riverbank, he searched for Rover but found no trace of him. The dog must have drowned and been swept downstream by the swift current. When the chow dog took up with Floyd, he was given the name Obie as a reminder of the long-lost Rover.

When I found Obie waiting at the entrance, I knew Floyd was inside. Perhaps he had taken a notion to explore and would not be out until morning. Then, too, he might be working on the trail—it would be just like him to go on working, regardless of the time, until the job was finished. I hesitated for a moment, then decided to look inside. There was no sign of him as far as the Grand Canyon, so I turned out the Crystal Route and began calling his name. If he had gone out any side leads, there was no chance of his hearing me. Furthermore, I would not know in which side passage to look unless he had left some indication, which was not likely. Each time I stopped to listen, the silence hung on me like a heavy weight. At the tunnel I thought I heard a reply.

"Hello, Floyd!" I shouted, "hurry through the tunnel."

"That's my old buddy Homer coming," he answered. "My light gave out. I been in the dark here for several hours."

"Where's your lantern?" I asked.

"It's back on the other side of the Dripping Spring."

"How on earth did you make it this far in the dark? It's mighty rough between here and there."

"I just got on my knees and crawled."

He went on to explain that he had been working on the path in the Crystal Route and was ready to leave the cave when he became interested in a hole at the side of the passage and began digging. He forgot that he had no spare light until the lantern went out. Floyd was not worried, for he was in the main passage, and Obie would stay at the entrance, giving notice that he was inside. He made himself comfortable, expecting a long wait, but he was dressed lightly and soon began to shiver.

I suppose the odds against feeling one's way along a big, rugged cave passage without light are about a million to one. Floyd did not want to spend the night shivering, so he tried it. He made it to the spring, skirted the pit, and entered the Devil's Kitchen. From there on the going was rough. To keep from falling he had to stay on his hands and knees. Once he wandered off the path and had trouble finding it again. He tossed rocks to the sides and to the front, trying to form a picture of the passage, judging distances by the time it took the rocks to hit. In this way he could detect the steep slopes and judge the nature of the floor from the sound. He had inched forward like this for several hours.

"It was kind of slow going," he said. "I'd probably have gotten mixed up at the Grand Canyon though."

Perhaps Floyd would have made it to the entrance by himself if I had not gone in after him. One thing is for certain—he would have made the world's biggest effort trying it.

When we came out, Obie was still waiting.

"If it hadn't been for old Obie, you'd still be in there feeling your way," I said.

Years later, Obie was to have a much longer wait.

Floyd had the cave ready for tourists by April, 1918. He enjoyed showing his discovery to the public, and many of the formations were named by tourists. The crystal flower garden reminded one visitor of her Grandma Ramsey's flower garden, so

Floyd's father Lee Collins in the Flower Garden.
Photo by Russell T. Neville. CRF Collection.

we called it Nanny Ramsey's Flower Garden. The gypsum-covered wall that looked like brown sugar was called Hoover's Sugar Reserve Wall in honor of Herbert Hoover, Food Administrator during World War I.

Our biggest problem was getting the public from the main highway to the cave, as the only road was a wagon trail. Only a horse could negotiate the mud holes, rocks and ruts that marked its hilly route. The county would not give us any aid in building a road, so we started working on it ourselves. Fortunately, there was a gravel deposit about two miles from home. Still, it took us about three years to make it usable year around. The farmers nearby hauled wagon loads of logs and cross-ties over it, cutting deep ruts. We had to work on the road constantly, especially when it rained.

Then trouble developed over the location of Crystal Cave. The boundary between Edmonson and Hart counties ran through our property, and so we were taxed by both counties—an amount far greater than we could afford. My father said that he would gladly sell the cave for the amount at which it was assessed, but the officials told him they were not in the market for buying caves; their business was to see that taxes were paid. Pap mortgaged his property and paid the taxes.

Floyd decided to buy an automobile to haul tourists from the highway to the cave. In the year 1918, there were practically no cars around home. Few people could afford one, and the roads just weren't made for automobile travel. Floyd dipped into his savings and bought a Crow-Elkhart five passenger touring car from Lem Ferguson. There was nothing else like it in the region. The Crow-Elkhart, now long forgotten, was made by a company in Elkhart, Indiana, and it was about the only car in the cave region that could get up the big hill between Crystal Cave and Mammoth Cave. More than one driver broke an axle on the rough road before it was better surfaced. Floyd was very proud of his car, but did not know how to drive. My brother Marshall had learned to drive and was going to teach him. They took the car out and Marshall began instructing Floyd, who was very eager to learn, so eager, in fact, that before his schooling was finished he took the car out by himself to show that he could drive without help. He started it all right, and drove away without any trouble, but there was an ominous roar as he came back into view over the rise about one hundred yards from the house. He was driving very fast. Suddenly, the car veered off the road, heading straight into the cornfield. Floyd clung to the wheel, frozen, as the car went on, speed undiminished. He cut a wide path through the cornfield, then headed for the barn. At least it cannot be said of Floyd that he could not hit the broad side of a barn; he smashed into it, tearing a gaping hole in the side, but was not hurt himself.

EIGHT

Helictite Gallery

Now that Floyd had a business to manage, a road to build, and a farm to work, it would seem that there would be no time left for caving. But Floyd's curiosity about caves continued, and he would sometimes cave at night after his day's work was done. He also worked from time to time at the Bluegrass Country Club. This club, owned by the Allied Golf Company of Chicago, was built by a group of Chicago businessmen on a tract of land about a mile west of home on the opposite side of the valley. Floyd frequently did odd jobs around the club and was even invited to play golf. Much to the surprise of those who invited him, he played a very good game. He was always good at swinging a club, whether it was a golf club or a baseball bat, and he was even handier at swinging an ax.

In 1919, Floyd was hired by the club to reopen Pike Chapman's Entrance to Great Salts Cave. The shaft had fallen in and was filled with rocks. Remembering Pike Chapman's death, few men cared to work in the shaft, so Floyd had Marshall, Andy Lee,

Floyd Collins wearing Great Crystal Cave pennant. *Photo by Wade Highbaugh. CRF Collection.*

Helictites in Crystal Cave. *Photo by Russell T. Neville. CRF Collection.*

and me help him. He decided to work from above and below, as in opening the entrance to Crystal Cave. The natural entrance to Great Salts Cave was a mile from the shaft as the crow flies. We carried a heavy wooden wheelbarrow through the rugged cave passage from the natural entrance to the bottom of the shaft. It took about two weeks to open the shaft, after which the sides were timbered to prevent collapse, and a stairway was built inside. Floyd used to guide parties from the club through the cave. Eventually, the club folded, and the shaft was filled once more. The old timbers, rotted and covered with moss, can still be seen at the site of the shaft wedged in among the boulders.

Floyd continued to explore Crystal Cave, pushing its boundaries farther and deeper into the ridge. He used to speculate on the true extent of the Grand Canyon, which apparently ended in a hill of clay and rock that rose all the way to the ceiling. He felt that the passage went beyond the clay fill, just as it extended beyond the first breakdown that stopped him before. At the end of the passage, there was a small crevice between the ceiling and the clay fill. The crevice was not large enough for Floyd to squeeze through, so he decided to follow it by digging his way along. His purpose was to find another Grand Canyon on the other side of the fill; the big question was how far the fill extended. He had learned from Edmund Turner that passages did not suddenly end in the center of the ridge, any more than a creek might be expected to begin in the middle of a field without any gullies, springs or other sources feeding it. And so he began digging, confident that he would find a big gallery on the other side of the fill.

For several hundred feet he squirmed through on his belly, enlarging the crevice just enough to

The wooden wheelbarrow Floyd used to open the Helictite Gallery. *Photo by Roger E. McClure.*

The Banana Stalk, helictites in Crystal Cave.
Photo by Russell T. NEville. CRF Collection.

Floyd Collins (arrow) with Neville party in Crystal Cave, 1924. *Photo by Russell T. Neville. CRF Collection.*

squeeze his body forward. The fill was more extensive than he had thought, but the few inches that separated it from the ceiling gave him something to follow. In places there were large rocks blocking the way. In his position it was difficult to work, but he had much patience. Slowly he would break rocks into small pieces or dig around them and, mole-like, inch forward. The distance kept piling up behind him, and still it looked no better ahead. His hopes for a quick breakthrough were gone.

Finally, Floyd met a new kind of obstacle, onyx formation in the passage. At first, it appeared to be only a small stalactite, but when he came closer, he saw it was a helictite. Helictites are a rare form of cave onyx that seems to defy the law of gravity. They twist and turn like pretzels, and sometimes stand out, horizontally, unlike stalactites and stalagmites, which are vertical. Beyond that point, the passage opened up and the formations became larger and more concentrated. Then he found the helictite grotto. The ceiling was pure white and the formations white, orange, and brown. There was nothing to equal this in the cave region. And the passage went on.

The discovery of the helictites was of far greater importance, from a business standpoint, than the extension of the Grand Canyon. Floyd immediately laid plans to show the new discovery to the public. The crawlway between the Grand Canyon and the helictites had to be dug out to standing height. The fill was of ocher, a clay used in pigments. It was packed too hard for him to dig with a shovel, so he first loosened it with a pick and then shoveled it into an old wooden wheelbarrow. Then he hauled it out to the canyon and dumped it over the hill. The job was too much for one man, and we all helped him. All winter we worked on the tunnel, and Helictite Gallery was open to the public when the summer tourist season began. The old wheelbarrow can be seen today at the beginning of the tunnel.

People are amazed at the work Floyd did with his crude methods, but they sometimes give him too much credit. Occasionally, a tourist asks, "Did those Collins boys dig out the Grand Canyon?" Or, seeing the great expanse of the flat ceiling, "Did Floyd plaster that ceiling?"

The opening of the new route was a success, the future looked bright, and Floyd was very happy guiding tourists through the cave. He had long known the satisfaction of finding a world no other man might ever see. Now he found equal satisfaction in showing his discoveries to the public.

NINE

Cave War

At first our house served as an office, but as the number of visitors increased, we had to have a separate building to take care of them. Floyd, a pretty good carpenter, built a ticket office that was completed in 1921 and is still in use today. Then, to accommodate overnight visitors, I put up a rooming house in 1922. It was a two-story, twelve-room frame building. Floyd and I occupied two rooms and rented the others. My sister, Nellie, cleaned the linens, but the visitors had to take care of the rooms themselves.

Our biggest problem still was to get tourists from the highway to the cave. Each of the commercial caves in the region had solicitors who went out on the road to sell tickets and give information. Those nearest the highway had the advantage; we were farthest from the beaten track. I ran a taxi service to Crystal Cave and solicited around the Mammoth Cave Hotel. They tried to keep me away from Mammoth Cave, saying I was running moonshine in my taxi. The charge was never proven.

Floyd Collins surrounded by specimens from Crystal Cave. *Photo from Howard W. Hartley's* Tragedy of Sand Cave.

The road at the entrance to Mammoth Cave was a country road. Since it was not private property, the roadside was lined with vendors and solicitors. Old one-eyed Joe Lee used to sell souvenirs there. Floyd did most of his soliciting there and sold souvenirs, too. He set up a stand displaying crystals and gypsum flowers, and when the tourists stopped to admire the formations, he told them of Crystal Cave. Usually they came over to see it, for Floyd had a flare for description.
   Now that the business was well established, Floyd was put under pressure to sell out. Pap was willing , but Floyd was determined to make a go of it. He was convinced that the cave would someday become world famous. Of course, there were hundreds of caves in the region, many of them commercialized. Competition was, and still is, very keen. But Floyd was determined to fight the competition.
   Once, when business slacked in the middle of the busy season, Floyd set out to find the reason. He discovered one of our competitors telling tourists that Crystal Cave was closed. We were so far back in the sticks that there was little chance of their coming over to find out. We had to reach them first and inform them before they were misled. That was one duty of the solicitor. But soliciting was sometimes dangerous, and a man who went out on the road had to be on his guard.
   Sometimes our road was blocked by wagons left there "accidentally" by a forgetful farmer. The road was narrow, and it was impossible to drive around the wagons. At other times there were boulders on the road, or big holes appeared overnight.
   One Saturday in 1924, I went to Bonnieville, twenty miles away, to visit a girlfriend. Her folks

invited me to stay overnight. Sunday morning after church, I started for home. At the crossroads, about a mile from home, a neighbor called to me. "Sorry to hear about the fire, Homer."

"What fire?" I asked.

"The one at your place," he said. "Didn't you know?"

"It's new to me."

"Why, your house burned down last night."

When I reached home, the charred remains of the rooming house lay smoldering on the ground. The barn also burned down. Floyd had been across the river visiting a friend, and no one was at home when it happened. We never discovered the cause of the fire.

One day I went to the mill for a wagon-load of lumber. It was wintertime and there were no tourists around. Floyd was in the house when five men drove up. They stepped out of the car and called him. Floyd, thinking it was a friendly visit, came out to meet them. A man who had approached Floyd numerous times on the matter of getting a lease on the cave was in charge of the group. They told Floyd to sign the lease. Floyd refused to sign, and they crowded close to him, but he stood his ground and ordered them off the property. The leader was furious.

"All right, Collins, you've stalled me long enough. I'm tired of this foolishness!" One of the men drew a gun. The others held Floyd while the leader slapped him across the face. "You'll sign or I'll beat you to death!"

Floyd defied them.

"Okay," the leader said. "You asked for it."

They began beating Floyd. Most of the blows

landed on his face and head. Blood ran over his face. Still he would not give in.

Meanwhile, I was returning from the mill with my wagon-load of lumber. There was a rise in the road just before the house. As I drove the wagon over the rise, I saw the men standing in the field in front of the house and the car parked alongside the road. At first I wondered who could be visiting us. Then, as I drew closer, I saw they were holding Floyd at gunpoint and beating him. They saw me and I knew it would be useless for me to run at them unarmed. They were on the far side of the house from me, so I jumped off the wagon and ran for the back door of the house. I wanted to kill them.

I kept a thirty-two Smith and Wesson revolver in the house. I ran out the front door with the gun in my hand, and they piled into their car, leaving Floyd dazed in the field. As they pulled away, I fired at them and ran after the car. The road was in such bad condition from the winter's freezing and thawing that they could not drive very fast, so I followed them, firing until my ammunition was gone. Several shots hit the car. I had run a mile down the road before giving up the chase. Then my reason took over, and I ran back to help Floyd. When I reached the house, he was still somewhat dazed by the beating, but not seriously hurt. After treating his cuts, we walked to Munfordville, twelve miles away, to swear out a warrant for the arrest of the gang. We reported the incident, but the men were never brought to court. Floyd was determined not to be driven out of business by violence. We prepared ourselves for future visits.

TEN

THE LOWER LEVELS

Floyd, like Edmund Turner, found cave business much rougher than cave exploring. But he was a shrewd businessman, and his bank account showed it. I do not recall anyone getting the best of him in a deal. He found one compensation for the difficulties of the business—meeting people. Each tourist was an interesting individual to him, a potential friend. This, and his enthusiasm about the cave, made him a very good guide. Many guides become bored and deliver their spiel like a phonograph record. Floyd spoke in earnest. He wanted people to appreciate the cave as he did, and he took their praises of his discovery as personal compliments. One of the friends Floyd made was Mrs. Emmons Blaine of Chicago, daughter of John McCormack. She sent Floyd a book on King Tut's tomb. He had been following the accounts of that discovery and had mentioned it to her when she visited Crystal Cave. Mrs. Blaine did not forget Floyd, and she sent help to him when he was trapped in Sand Cave.

Floyd was now in his thirties. He had been caving

since he was six. Floyd could not stop while there remained a question mark in any passage. The big question mark in Crystal Cave was the absence of lower level passages. All the passages Floyd had found so far were on a high level. He knew there was a large system of caverns with an underground river somewhere below the commercial routes. The

Floyd Collins, cave guide, with tourists at Crystal Cave. *Photo from Howard W. Hartley's* Tragedy of Sand Cave.

river was evident from the great volume of water in Pike Spring, only a few hundred yards from the cave entrance. He could not follow the spring, however, for the passage from which it issued was completely submerged. Floyd tried working into the lower levels through openings on the hillside near the Green River, but he could not break into the main system. He probed every opening that he could find inside the cave, pits, crevices, crawlways, and breakdowns. The hole at Scotchman's Trap, near the end of the Crystal Route about a quarter mile beyond the Devil's Kitchen, led him into an extensive system of crawlways and narrow canyons. There seemed to be no end to this maze of small passages. Floyd felt that if he followed these crawlways far enough, he would find the lower levels.

In his search for the lower levels of Crystal Cave, Floyd was not trying to establish another commercial route. There was enough on the upper levels to satisfy the tourists. It was curiosity, not necessity, that kept him exploring. And in these remote passages, with only a kerosene lantern for company, he found adventure.

Floyd followed the crawlway at Scotchman's Trap to a canyon that intersects it at right angles. He chose the right-hand branch. The canyon was so narrow he had to turn sideways to follow it. Then the passage changed to a knee-crawl. The sharp-edged rocks cut into his flesh and ripped his trouser legs. The sand added to the irritation. The passage became smaller. His back scraped the ceiling, and he dropped flat. Now he was in a belly-crawl. He shoved his lantern ahead, dug in with the toes of his boots and pushed, dug in with his fingers and pulled. Then he came to an S-shaped curve. Here

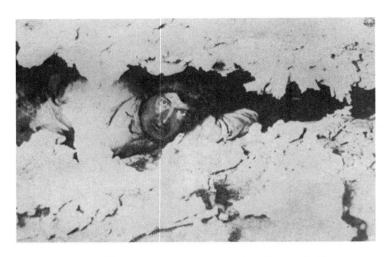

Floyd Collins in a crawlway in Cyrstal Cave.
Photo from Howard W. Hartley's
Tragedy of Sand Cave.

the passage fit his body like a glove. Pushing and pulling were not enough. He wiggled and twisted, moving through the S-curve like a snake, turning his face sideways to keep from eating dirt.

If you have the slightest tendency toward claustrophobia, it will show in a place like this. Your body touches the rock on all sides. It is like being held in a gigantic vise. The crawlway is a delicate thread of air, winding its way through the massive rocks, at the mercy of tectonic forces. You feel weak, insignificant. But you are elated, for in spite of your weakness, you have penetrated this labyrinth. And there is the constant hope that beyond the next obstacle lies a discovery.

Floyd snaked through the S-curve and crawled on. Then he saw a small hole to his left and a slightly larger passage to his right. He poked his head through the small hole, but it seemed to be too small for his body. There was solid rock on all sides, with no possibility of digging. He squeezed in until his chest stuck in the hole. Then he braced his feet against the opposite wall, exhaled, and pushed. A little scraping against the rocks and he was through.

He had entered a T-shaped passage that was low and wide at the top, with a narrow canyon beneath. Intersecting passages became more numerous. Floyd marked his way with little rock piles. Even an experienced explorer cannot rely on memory alone to retrace his steps. The passages look different from one direction than from the other. Side passages not seen on the way in may be the most obvious on the way out. There are many holes to go through, and many others that look just like them. In these long crawlways, Floyd had to sacrifice equipment for mobility. If his supply of light gave out, he was helpless. He could not afford to waste time searching for the right leads on the way out.

Floyd came to a room about thirty feet across. The floor was a jumbled mass of breakdown rock. Off to one side he could hear water, and the rocks were damp all around. He climbed over the rocks on the side toward the water and lowered himself about six feet to a damp passage with a canyon running underneath. He stayed at the top, straddling the canyon, until he came to another room. To get into the room, he climbed down between the walls of the canyon, for there was a crumbly ledge across the top that might have given way under him. Beyond that point the cave opened into a maze of big passageways, pits, streams—a whole new system to explore. He had found the lower levels of Crystal Cave.

One day in the year 1922, my brother Marshall

and I went with Floyd to Scotchman's Trap. Marshall's wife, Anne, did not want to be left behind. She donned an old pair of overalls and joined the party. We had not planned anything strenuous and carried only two lanterns for the four of us. At Scotchman's Trap, Floyd and I went into the crawlway, but Anne decided to wait there until we returned. Marshall didn't want her to sit there alone, so he stayed with her. I asked Marshall to let me use his lantern in the crawlway. He didn't mind sitting in the dark with Anne. I took the lantern, assuring them I wouldn't be gone long, and followed Floyd through the crawlway. I stayed at his heels, bumping against the rocks and eating dirt to keep him in sight. We were about the same size, but he had a knack of slithering through crawlways, seeming to use every muscle in his body as he moved along. And he never wasted a motion. If he put his hand on a rock, it was the best point of support. His body was always in the best position for the contour of the passage at any point. I was too busy trying to keep up with him to take note of any of the route. All I saw was heels, lantern, and dust. Finally, we came to the room with the crumbly ledge, where it is necessary to climb down. I suggested we turn around. Floyd wanted to go on. "Come on Homer, there's no use turning back now."

"Let's wait until we've got a rope along," I said. "Beside, it's time we headed out."

Floyd disliked turning back as long as he had enough light to go on. If he ever tired, he didn't show it. A crawl, a climb, or a breakdown, these obstacles were a challenge. Only the problem of light overcame his enthusiasm to keep going. He tried to urge me on. "Come on, Homer, this is an easy climb."

"No, Floyd, Anne and Marshall are waiting in the dark. If you don't come with me, I'm going back alone."

I finally persuaded him to leave. When we came out of the crawlway at Scotchman's Trap, Marshall and Anne were gone. They had no light, and they were not likely to feel their way out as Floyd had done. We walked all the way to the Dripping Spring without finding a sign of them. At every turn, we expected to find them groping along on their hands and knees.

After we had left Marshall and Anne, they had made themselves comfortable and waited in the dark. Marshall began to worry when we did not return as I had promised. He thought we might have had an accident—perhaps we needed help. Time passes very slowly sitting in darkness in a cave, waiting. Marshall had some matches in his pocket, but not enough to reach the entrance. He took off his coat and made a torch of it. By the light of the burning coat, they could see well enough to find their way. We caught up with them in time to save Marshall from an uncomfortable situation, for at the rate he was burning his clothing he would have been nude by the time he reached the entrance.

Floyd and I prepared for another trip to the lower levels. We started out early in the morning with two hundred feet of rope and plenty of oil for our lanterns. I made it through the crawlway with a good deal of sweating and grunting, dragging the extra load. Most cavers today wear small carbide lights hooked to their hats, a great improvement over the clumsy kerosene lanterns we pushed in front of us.

Out of the crawlway, we climbed down the wall at the room where we had stopped before and went through a small crevice to a high, narrow passage.

We skirted the edge of a pit where the passages intersected. A few feet from there we came to a pit and dome off to the side of the passage. After a heavy rain, the trickle of water coming out of the dome becomes a roaring waterfall. It is called Ebb and Flow Falls. We had worked up quite a thirst in the crawlway, sweating and eating dust, so we stopped for a drink. Refreshed, we went on.

We straddled a deep canyon and then crawled through a few bottlenecks in the passage. Floyd, in the lead, was much more enthusiastic than I. He was fascinated by the extent of the cave. I was more interested in finding formations to attract the eye of a tourist. He saw beauty in this rough, barren passage. Others might only find it tiring.

We came to a pit over a hundred feet deep. Floyd began looking for a way down. He worked his way down through a nearby crevice. I followed close behind him. The crevice led him away from the pit, but he was getting lower all the time without having to use the rope. Near the bottom the walls belled out. The ceiling was out of sight.

In this room we heard water, evidently flowing very rapidly. On the far side of the room we dropped down about fifteen feet and found a stream cascading from a narrow crevice. Floyd went into the crevice to find the source of the stream. The sound of the water cascading over the rocks filled my ears as I followed him up the stream. I was busy trying to avoid the water and keep up with Floyd, while juggling my lantern as I braced myself on the slippery rocks. Then I thought I heard another sound, but the ears play tricks on you in a cave—especially in a passage like this. I moved forward a few steps, and then I heard the sound distinctly—a roar! Floyd had already found the source. He shouted back to me, "It's a waterfall!"

We were at the bottom of a large pit. The air was filled with mist and spray. Above, out of sight, a stream emptied into the pit. The column of water plummeted downward, dashed against the rocks, and ran off through the crevice. The reverberations created a continuous thunder in the rock chamber. We could not see the source of the stream by the light of our lanterns, because the top of the pit was lost in the darkness. We stood there soaked and shivering, Floyd thinking about the source of the stream, me thinking about the commercial value of the waterfall. There was nothing known like this in the cave region. It would make a great tourist attraction.

We had been in the cave nearly thirty hours, so we turned around and headed out. In the crawlway the sand stuck to our wet bodies. My knees were scarred from crawling over the jagged rocks, and the grinding sand irritated them. I duck-walked when the ceiling was not too low, and I crawled with as much weight on my arms as possible to save my shredded knees. Floyd was hardened to this. The climax of the trip now past, my enthusiasm gone, I could think only of my aching muscles, my sore knees, and the sand inside my clothing. Floyd was already planning new exploration. I wondered what drove him on, literally beating himself against the rocks. He would go back again and again to more crawlways, pits, and crevices. He would go alone. I wondered if it was worth it.

The return trip through the crawlway convinced me that the lower levels of Crystal Cave could not be shown to the public. To enlarge the crawlway, as we had done on the Helictite Route, would have been impractical—nearly impossible. Floyd agreed it could not be shown unless a shorter, more workable connection was found. The waterfall, for a time, was only for cavers.

ELEVEN

Floyd's Lost Passage

Floyd made may trips to the lower levels of Crystal Cave alone. His equipment was a kerosene lantern; his supplies, a can of beans. Sometimes he stayed for two and three days by himself, sleeping a few hours at a time on the cave floor where the passage was dry enough. Now, more then ever, he was thought curious by the neighbors. What normal man would wander alone below ground where, should anything happen, no one could ever find him? An athlete performs a task impossible for the normal man. We accept his performance, knowing that he has spent years in specialized training. Floyd's life had trained him for this kind of caving. He had gradually become accustomed to the feeling of being cut off from the world. The caverns were not gloomy or mysterious to him. He knew the risk of this lone caving, but the risk was the difference between a sight-seeing tour and an adventure.

On one trip to the lower levels, Floyd came to a ledge overlooking a large canyon passage. There was a drop of about eight feet onto a sloping pile of loose rock. He had no rope along, so he moved out on the ledge and looked for a place to jump. If he landed on the loose rock it would mean a twisted ankle or worse. Here, a sprained ankle was a serious matter. At the top of the slope, off to the side of the ledge, was a flat place. He scooted along the ledge in that direction until he began to slip, then jumped. He landed safely and went on to explore the passage.

When Floyd returned to the ledge, he could not climb up again. There were no hand holds. Furthermore, the ledge was rounded, making it impossible to jump up and grab it, even if it had been within jumping reach. There was no other way around that he could find. He began building a pyramid out of the rock fragments on the floor. It was slow work, but better than waiting for help in a place that only he knew about. Finally he was able to stand on top of the pyramid and reach over the ledge. Not only was the ledge rounded on the edge, but it was covered with sand and gravel. This made it difficult to use the friction of his body against the rock for a hold. Once he had began pulling himself up, it would be too late to drop back, for it had been necessary to build the pyramid a little off to the side. After his feet left the pyramid his body would swing out over the steep slope. He braced himself, then lurched forward. For a moment only his arms and chest were on the slippery ledge. The gravel flew as he scrambled upward. With no way to use his feet, he dug in with his fingers and elbows and wiggled over the ledge. After much clawing and twisting he drew himself to safety and went on his way. This drop, now a familiar landmark to explorers in Crystal Cave, is known as Floyd's Jump-Off.

Floyd pushed the boundaries of the cave farther

Floyd's bean and kerosene cans as he left them in
Floyd's Lost Passage, Crystal Cave.
Photo by Roger E. McClure.

and deeper. He found the system more complex than any he had ever seen. The passages wound around, crisscrossed, and seemed to go on endlessly. Then he discovered a big passage about a mile long in a very low level. It was different from any other passage in the cave. The floor was piled deep with sand, smooth as a beach. The walls and ceiling formed a wide, smooth arch. Floyd chose this as a camp site. The sand floor made good sleeping, and there were several springs for drinking water. He carried supplies to his camp on each trip. Some of the old bean cans, rusted through, can still be seen a few feet from Floyd's Spring. This spring was conveniently located beside a waist-high shelf of rock that made a fine dinner table. It is now called Floyd's Kitchen, and is still used as a dining table. A few hundred yards from the spring, Floyd found a gypsum flower garden even more spectacular than that on the upper level.

Gypsum flowers in Crystal Cave. *Photo by Russell T. Neville. CRF Collection.*

The petals were so long, he wondered why they didn't break off under their own weight. He took Wade Highbaugh, the Mammoth Cave photographer and night-school teacher, to the lower levels to photograph the flowers.

On one trip Floyd found a bare footprint in the damp floor of a side passage. Someone had gone through without shoes, probably an Indian. Where he came from and where he went was a mystery. The Indians had used reed torches for light, but no one could have come that far burning reeds. Maybe there was another way in. After Floyd died, no one could find the big passage with the gypsum flowers. Some doubted the existence of Floyd's Lost Passage. It was not rediscovered until 1941. Likewise the story of the bare footprint was scoffed at until 1954, when a number of bare footprints were found and photographed in remote parts of the cave.

For the expedition in 1954, a camp was set up on the sandy floor of Floyd's Lost Passage just two hundred yards from Floyd's Spring. Dozens of cavers bustled through the passages that Floyd had walked alone.

TWELVE

SAND CAVE

Floyd took several of his friends to the lower levels of Crystal Cave. One of his friends, Johnnie Geralds, was interested in getting an option on the cave. Johnnie, a tobacco buyer from Cave City, had known Floyd since boyhood. In the summer of 1924, Johnnie helped Floyd out of a tight spot in Crystal Cave. It happened while Floyd was showing John Vance and Johnnie through the cave. They were investigating a passage that leads off from the Devil's Kitchen, and very soon ran into a bad breakdown. John and Johnnie followed Floyd until it became too risky. Floyd wanted to go on, so they sat and waited while he probed the breakdown. The entire passage in front of him was filled with broken rock. He worked his way between the big blocks of limestone and was soon out of sight. As Johnnie and John sat on the rocks waiting, they heard a shout. They stopped talking and listened. Floyd was in trouble. "Come and get me out. I'm hung!"

Neither of the men had much desire to enter the breakdown, even though both of them had explored caves, because this breakdown just looked too dangerous. Nevertheless, Johnnie went in. He found Floyd unhurt, caught in an awkward position between the rocks. Johnnie freed him, and they returned to where John was waiting. The incident did not bother Floyd; he never mentioned it to me. He continued exploring by himself and did not avoid bad breakdown, any more than a driver who has scraped a fender avoids driving.

Friends and family warned Floyd that he was taking too many risks. He knew the risk far better than they did. There were still many unexplored leads in the lower levels, and he was not going to let the scare talk of his friends keep him from exploring them.

Meanwhile, Floyd was considering another commercial venture, not in Crystal Cave, but at the opposite end of the ridge. It was a nameless hole at the base of a bluff, one of the countless openings that dot the land in the cave region. This hole, which was to become known as Sand Cave, led to a narrow passage that twisted downward through loose rock and debris. A few men had gone a short distance, but it had proven too dangerous for them. Floyd suspected a cavern lay somewhere below; he was determined to work through the debris and find the cavern.

There were many caves in the area far less dangerous than this one. But Sand Cave was only a hundred yards from the highway, an ideal location for a commercial venture. Contrary to popular belief, Floyd was not looking for another entrance to Crystal Cave or Mammoth Cave. Floyd planned to operate Sand Cave if he found anything there. Tourists stopping to visit Sand Cave could be given information about Crystal Cave as well. At the close of the tourist season in 1924, he made plans for the exploration of the "hole near the highway."

Three pieces of property joined near the entrance to Sand Cave. The owners were Ed Estes, Bee Doyle, and Jesse Lee Cox. Floyd figured that the cave might lie under the land of all three men, therefore he made an agreement with the three of them to explore the cave. He was to get fifty percent of the income from anything he might discover there and the property owners would divide the other half among themselves. While he was working on the project, they were to take turns boarding him. This was the situation when he began work in mid-December, 1924.

Crystal Cave and Mammoth Cave lie in a bed of limestone some three hundred feet thick. Over the top of this limestone there is a layer of resistant sandstone caprock that acts as a protective covering for the caves. There are some openings in this caprock, but the caves are formed in the limestone underneath. There was sandstone at Sand Cave, and this was very dangerous material to work in, but Floyd was not worried. He knew that once the passage dropped down deep enough, he would get below the sandstone and into the cave-bearing limestone. This proved to be the case, for the passage did drop down into limestone just as he expected.

Around the foot of a cliff, there is usually found a sloping heap of rock fragments broken off from the hillside. This pile of broken rock, known as talus, accumulates as a result of the wearing away of the cliff over a period of thousands of years. The passage in which Floyd worked was on the edge of a talus slope. Although one wall was solid, the other was composed of loose material. Day after day, Floyd went down into the hole and removed the loose rock. He gradually extended the passage, working his way deeper and deeper into the ground. It was not a straight, tunnel-like passage, but varied in size and shape, and it changed direction every few feet. The first part of the passage had been explored by other men before Floyd and was not difficult to get through.

Floyd worked in the cave by himself. Each morning he would enter the hole, drop through the crevice, make his way through the tunnel, and crawl and slide down the corkscrew-like passage, until he reached the point where he had left off the day before. Then the digging would begin. All day he would lie in the mud and gravel, picking at the loose rock, moving forward inches at a time, and working in a cramped position at all times. Standing upright was a luxury to be enjoyed only when he left the cave. His only companions were the mud and the cold solid stone of the passage; his only comfort was the light of his lantern.

Granting all Floyd's past experience, you may still wonder how he was able to work under such conditions. Did it not bother him to be cut off from the world that way, hemmed in by stone and darkness, constantly threatened by the shifting rocks? The only answer I can give is that his mind was on his job. He worked tirelessly at the task before him, never giving his thoughts a chance to linger on these matters. He knew before entering the cave what dangers were to be faced and what precautions had to be taken. Once inside, his every thought and every effort were directed toward the task of exploration. He had to work steadily to overcome the obstacles in this path. There was no time for worry.

Only once did Floyd show any sign of being affected by the dangers of his work. One night he dreamed that he was trapped in a cave and could not get out. The dream was so vivid that he woke up sweating and struggling in his bed, and he was unable to go back to sleep that night. Such a dream might seem natural, considering the hazardous conditions in Sand Cave, but it was unusual for Floyd. On hearing about the dream, our stepmother, whom Pap had married after Mother's death, said that she had been feeling all along that something bad was going to happen to him. But Floyd was accustomed to such warnings, and he scoffed at the incident and continued his work.

The job turned out to be rather difficult. Weeks passed and Floyd still had not broken through into big cave. He encountered a narrow squeeze that slowed his progress considerably. Nevertheless, he went a little deeper each day. He did not become discouraged with the difficult task, for he had worked for long periods of time on crawlways in Crystal Cave and in many other places. He worked six days a week at Sand Cave, staying at the home of one of the three partners. On Sundays, he would spend the day at home with us, resting up for another grueling week underground. Six weeks passed in this manner.

Sunday, January 25, 1925, Floyd spent the day at home as was his custom. After working in the hole for so long, he felt certain that he would break through the following week. The next morning, he rose early, enthusiastic about the possibility of completing the job within the next few days. I had decided to make a trip to Louisville that same morning to buy a new car, so Floyd and I walked together

Floyd Collins. *Photo from Howard W. Hartley's* Tragedy of Sand Cave.

from Crystal Cave to the home of Ed Estes, where Floyd had stayed the week before. This was a distance of about five miles. It had begun to snow that morning, so I had put on a pair of heavy four-buckle boots. Floyd was wearing low-cut rubber overshoes. We wore the same size shoe, so I decided to give him the four-buckle boots, since I would not be needing them as much as he would.

As we walked over to Sand Cave, Floyd asked me if I would care to help him in opening the passage, since we had worked together so many times before. "I'm going to open a big cave any day now," he said. "Won't you stay and help me?" Looking back upon that moment now, I would give anything in the world to relive it so I could answer yes. But I was young, and buying a car seemed more important to me. A trip to Louisville was much more inviting than a grimy crawl into that dark, gloomy hole beneath the bluff. Furthermore, I had the greatest faith in Floyd's ability; there was no doubt in my mind that he could finish the job alone. I decided not to stay and help him.

We sat down in the snow and exchanged overshoes before parting. Floyd went on to finish his job, and I headed for town.

THIRTEEN

Trapped

After leaving Floyd at Sand Cave, I went in to the town of Horse Cave, where I intended to catch the train for Louisville. The train pulled out shortly before I arrived, so I strolled around town. I saw Floyd's friend, Johnnie Geralds, and we talked a little bit about Crystal Cave. That night, I stayed at his aunt's house, and I caught the train Tuesday morning. When I arrived in Louisville, I went to visit Mr. O. J. Branden, a friend of mine who kept me at his house while I stayed in town. On Wednesday, I bought a used car, but did not leave for home right away. I was still in Louisville on Friday, and when I went to bed Friday night I had trouble sleeping. All night I tossed and turned, unable to rest. Saturday morning, I made up my mind to return to Crystal Cave. "Mr. Branden," I said, "I've got to go home this morning."

He asked me to stay awhile longer. "The roads are awfully bad, Homer."

It was snowing and the highway was rather dangerous, but I felt restless and decided to return anyway. Driving my newly acquired automobile, I started for home, a distance of over a hundred miles. The road was covered with snow, so I drove very slowly. It took me the better part of the day to reach Cave City. This was the last day of January and night fell early; it was just beginning to get dark as I pulled into Cave City. My car was low on gas, so I pulled into a service station to fill up the tank before proceeding to Crystal Cave. I was wondering how Floyd would like the car I had bought, and as I sat there reflecting on the matter, my thoughts were rudely interrupted by a young boy who shouted in the window. "Have you got your brother out of the cave yet?"

These words came like an explosion. I was stunned. "What?" I said.

He told me that Floyd was trapped in a cave, but at last word he was still alive. At once I started up my car and drove at full speed toward Sand Cave.

On the Monday that Floyd and I parted, he went to the home of Ed Estes to pick up the work clothes he had left there the week before. He was to board with Bee Doyle that week. He gathered his equipment and started on another week of digging. Floyd was determined to get into a cavern below the tortuous crevice before the end of the week. There was still a great deal of debris to be cleared out of the narrow squeeze. He labored for hours at a time, lying in the cold muck, to finish the job. His determination to complete the task drove him to almost superhuman effort.

Along about the middle of the week, Floyd spent almost thirty hours working in the hole without coming out. Doyle knew that Floyd often stayed underground for long periods of time, but after twenty-four hours, Doyle became alarmed, because he knew that this cave was especially dangerous. He went down to the entrance and called to Floyd, who was still hard at work inside. Floyd told him that everything was all right, he merely wanted to finish the job before coming out. Doyle left him there with a word of warning and climbed back up the hill to the house.

After Doyle left, Floyd returned to his task. At the farthest end of the passage, there was a small vertical chimney, about ten feet from top to bottom, where Floyd had been working. He finally managed to enlarge this crevice sufficiently to squeeze through, and on reaching the bottom he found a little cubbyhole about the size of a salt barrel. Squatting in that small space, he saw that there was another crevice below him. This crevice was not vertical, but sloped downward at a steep angle, apparently dropping off into a large cavern. The space was much too small for him to get through, and there were many loose rocks overhead. He felt that this was the last obstacle standing between him and the big cave he had been seeking. But it would require the utmost caution to get past this point. Before returning to the surface for a badly needed rest, Floyd surveyed the situation to see what would be required the following day.

Friday morning, January 30, Floyd informed Doyle at the breakfast table that this was the final day. Before nightfall the cave would be open. Floyd was very excited as he anticipated the discovery; Doyle was more concerned about his partner's safety. Floyd told him that he had cleared out most of the loose rock the day before, and on this trip it would merely be a matter of squeezing through that final crevice into the big cave. Doyle cautioned him repeatedly about taking risks, but Floyd was too happy with his success to be worried.

It was about seven o'clock in the morning when Floyd entered the cave for the final push. Crawling and sliding down the rock-strewn passage, he worked his way deep into the ground. Twenty minutes later, he arrived at the top of the small hole that led down to the cubbyhole and the final crevice. He tied a rope to a projecting rock in the section of tunnel just above the hole. There was no need for the rope yet, for despite all his digging, the hole was so narrow that he had to force his way down. But he would need the rope for the drop-off into the cavern he had seen below the final crevice. He started into the hole above the cubbyhole feet first, forcing his way down until he was in that barrel-like space. Imagine climbing down a chimney no bigger around than your own body, lined with projecting rocks that dig into your flesh and tear your clothing. This is the sort of thing he had to squeeze through before arriving at the cubbyhole. Then the real work began.

Squatting in the cubbyhole for a brief rest (if this can be called resting), he surveyed the situation before starting on the last leg of his downward journey. He fed his rope through the opening, moved a few rocks out of the way, then tugged on the rope for one last check before starting into the crevice. Now he began to work his way through, again traveling feet first. He had to shove with all his might to get through, but at the same time feel his way with extreme care lest he dislodge some of the loose rocks. The sound of gravel bouncing over the rocks below him gave notice of the drop he was approaching.

The occasional crash of a larger rock, dislodged by his feet, resounded through the cavern. Like the opening above the cubbyhole, this one, too, was no larger than his own body. He could not see into the cavern below him, for his own body was in the way. The rocks pulled at his clothing, making it difficult to force himself downward. At the same time, he had to hold the rope, ready for the moment he emerged from the crevice to make the descent into the cavern.

He noticed that there were some rather large loose rocks overhead. He lay beneath a huge limestone boulder weighing several tons, but this did not bother him, as it was wedged solidly in place. But beneath that boulder he saw a smaller rock. It weighed less than a hundred pounds, but it gave him some concern. This rock appeared to be rather loose, and it hung in a very narrow part of the opening through which he had to pass. He took the greatest care not to dislodge it. He proceeded cautiously, until at last his body was free of the binding crevice.

Grasping the rope in his hands, he quickly lowered himself to the floor of the cavern. His excitement mounted as he found himself in a good-sized space. Looking back up the slope he had just come down, he thought it incredible that he could have come through that small crack in the ceiling where the rope disappeared. Judging from the amount of rope he had payed out, he figured that he had dropped down about eighty feet. Then he began to investigate the cave. He looked about for some sign of formations, but did not find any. The walls were barren, and he thought they looked smoked. However, he was not certain of this. If they were, perhaps it was from the torches used by Indians who had inhabited the cave, or this passage might be connected with Mammoth Cave, where guides had used torches while guiding parties through the cave.

As he looked around, the thrill of discovery made him forget the weeks of labor he had spent getting into this cavern. To you who have never explored, this momentary thrill may seem to be small compensation for the amount of work and the risk involved. It is impossible for anyone else to understand the feelings of a man like Floyd on making such a discovery. The thrill of standing in virgin cave after overcoming the obstacle that has hidden it throughout the ages, this is the great reward.

While Floyd was engaged in examining the cavern, his light flickered. His thoughts returned to the more practical aspects of exploration. He shook the lantern and found that it still contained some kerosene, but the light flickered again. He decided that he had better leave. Turning toward the entrance, he thought of the reception awaiting him when he told Bee Doyle of the cave that he found. He reached the slope and started the climb up to the crack in the ceiling, through which he had to squeeze before starting the crawl toward the entrance. He had no trouble climbing up from the floor of the cavern. He did not really need the rope, as there were enough projections on the wall to make the climb without it. However, he pulled himself up and arrived in a few seconds at the hole in the ceiling. Now he began the difficult task of getting himself up into the narrow crevice. It was a slow process, and he was anxious to be out of the cave to tell the farmers of his discovery. Holding the lantern in front of him, he pulled himself into the opening with all his might. He slowly drew himself upward so he could lie on the floor of the crevice. In the narrow crevice, it was impossible for Floyd to carry his lantern. He pushed it in front of him as far as possible, set it down, then followed behind. The cubbyhole was now almost within reach. Before advancing the last few feet, however, he had first to push the lantern through. He managed to shove it into the open space, but the lantern fell on its side. The light went out, and he was left in the darkness.

Although he was in a precarious situation, Floyd did not become excited. He figured that he would be able to light the lantern again as soon as he got up into the cubbyhole. If not, he would have to feel his way out. His only concern at that moment was to get out of the crevice in which he was wedged. The shape of the crevice was such that he had to place his arms at his side in order to move forward. Bracing his feet against the rocks, he pushed, twisting and turning, seeking the best position for his body to move forward. His face was pressed hard against the rocks as he struggled to advance. Straining with all his might, he kicked out with his right foot and struck a loose rock that hung over his legs. It was the same rock that had given him some concern on the way in. It had been hanging there with its pointed end downward, ready to fall at the slightest disturbance. Without warning, the rock broke loose and fell.

Floyd's left leg was at the bottom of a V-shaped crevice, and the rock, pointed end downward, lodged in the crevice just above his ankle. He was not hurt, but his foot was caught by the fallen rock, and he was unable to move. The rock itself was not very large; it weighed less than a hundred pounds.

But it was wedged tight. His foot would not slide past it. Floyd's right foot was still free and he used it to try and kick himself loose. It seemed that the more he kicked, the more firmly wedged the rock became. At the same time, his kicking dislodged some more rocks from above, trapping his right foot as well as the left. Floyd was anxious to be out of the cave, and this hindrance irritated him. Again, he tried to draw his foot past the rock, but the heavy boots he was wearing prevented him from doing so. He was not able to move backwards to shove the rock into the room, because he was wedged in too tightly. His arms were pinned at his side, so he could not reach out in front of him to help draw himself upward. His struggles were useless—each movement seemed to wedge him tighter. He stopped to consider the situation more calmly.

Floyd realized that he was going to need help. It was about 10 o'clock in the morning, and he would not be missed until that night. Even then, Bee Doyle was not likely to come after him, knowing that Floyd was accustomed to staying underground for long periods of time. It was cold and wet in the crevice. The jagged rocks made it impossible for him to lie in a comfortable position. It was bad enough to lie there for even a few minutes. Floyd dreaded the long hours ahead of him. If only he could remove his boot, he thought, there would be a chance of drawing his foot past the rock. That would mean torn flesh, but it would be better than lying there in the darkness for hours, perhaps days, waiting for help. However, he could not reach his boots. In the meantime, every movement brought loose material sliding into the crevice, solidly packing the space around his body. His hands were torn from clawing at the rocks, his muscles were sore from the strenuous effort, and his body ached from the cramped position and the jagged rocks on which he was lying. When he stopped struggling, he could hear the beating of his heart. The deathly silence was broken occasionally by the clatter of gravel falling into the cavern below. The sound was magnified; it reverberated through the rocky prison for a moment, then left it in silence again.

Realizing that all motion was futile, Floyd now spent most of his time lying still, praying. He would have to wait until someone came down to free him. The hours passed, but he had no idea of the time. Minutes seemed like hours. The rocks were hard, the dampness penetrating, and the darkness heavy. He waited and prayed.

FOURTEEN

The Rescue Begins

Friday night, Bee Doyle waited anxiously for Floyd to return from the cave. He finally concluded that Floyd must be working overtime to clear the final obstacles, since he had been so confident that morning of entering big cave. Doyle went to bed, but found it difficult to sleep. He was very much worried about Floyd, and a storm outside added to his uneasiness. Thunder and lightning kept Doyle turning restlessly in his bed.

Saturday morning, he rose and checked to see if Floyd had come in during the night. The bed had not been slept in. Doyle was somewhat alarmed. Before eating breakfast, he hurried over to the house of Ed Estes. Floyd had not been there either. Estes took the matter more calmly and tried to reassure Doyle. Floyd was experienced, he knew how to take care of himself, he would show up all right. Doyle returned home and ate breakfast. His fears grew stronger. Immediately after breakfast, he went to Estes' house again. Doyle convinced him this time that they should check on Floyd to see if he was in trouble. Estes called his son Jewel, who was seventeen, and the three men headed for the cave. On arriving at the entrance, they found Floyd's coat and hat on the ledge outside. Jewel was slender and

Jewel Estes, age 17, the first person to reach Floyd Collins in Sand Cave. *Photo by Russell T. Neville. CRF Collection.*

strong, capable of traversing the difficult passage, so he led the way into the cave. The older men made it to the beginning of the first tight squeeze in the passage, where they waited while Jewel went ahead. The young boy, unaccustomed to crawling through rough caves, showed courage in going forward alone. He finally succeeded in reaching a point where he was able to talk to Floyd.

Floyd had been lying in the damp crevice, helpless, for twenty-four hours, his left foot held tight by the stone that had fallen on it, and his body nearly covered with gravel. Unable to sleep, he had waited in silence, listening for the sound of his rescuers. Occasionally he had tried to free himself, even though he knew it was useless, for it is difficult to lie still, in pain, shivering from the cold, and do nothing. He prayed that someone would come after him, wondering how much time had passed and how long it would take. Then he heard Jewel's voice. Rescuers! It would be a short time now. He quickly explained the situation, assuring Jewel that he could get out all right with a little help. "Get my brothers over here," he said, "and tell them to bring some boys over with them."

Jewel hurried back to tell the news to his father, and the three men left the cave to go for help. Doyle and Estes rode to Crystal Cave on mules and informed my father that Floyd was trapped. Pap called Marshall, who was in the house at the time, and the four men started back to Sand Cave. Valuable hours were slipping past. A telegram was sent to Louisville to call me home. Meanwhile I was already on the road, unaware of the accident.

It was noon when Doyle, Estes, Marshall, and Pap reached the cave. A crowd had already gathered around the entrance. Marshall quickly organized a rescue party and they entered the hole. Of those who accompanied Marshall, only Louis Brown stayed with him all the way. Louis was a Negro who worked as a "trailer" at Mammoth Cave, bringing up the rear of touring parties to see that no stragglers became separated from the rest of the party. When Marshall finally contacted Floyd, although they were separated by more than twenty feet, he could not find the place where Floyd had gone down.

"I don't see any hole," Marshall said. "How did you get down there?"

"You must be in the wrong place," Floyd answered.

Marshall went back about twenty feet to a tunnel that was about ten feet higher than Floyd's head, and he found a hole where Floyd had been digging. There was a bag full of sand on the floor of the passage at that point. Marshall started into this hole, but soon found that it came to a dead end where Floyd had stopped digging. He backed out of this blind alley and called to Floyd again. "I went into one hole up here, but it's blocked up."

"Was there a sandbag where you went in?" Floyd asked.

"Yes."

"Well, that's the wrong place. I was using that sandbag to kneel on while I dug there, but I gave that hole up after awhile. Come back to the other end of the tunnel and you'll find a narrow crevice that's just about over my head; it's a little pit about ten feet deep. Be careful as you come down it. Don't knock any rocks on me."

Marshall found the crevice and peered down into it, but still could not see Floyd, who was hidden beneath a ledge of rock. "It looks to me like this thing has fallen in some, Floyd; I can't get through it. Don't worry, though, We'll dig it out and get down to you."

And so the rescue work began. Marshall and Louis Brown stayed there digging without letup the rest of the day, gradually enlarging the crevice. Marshall had been sick and was in no condition to be working in the cold muck, but he would not leave the cave. Saturday afternoon passed, and still they were not able to squeeze through the small hole leading down to Floyd. This crevice just above his head was no more than ten feet from top to bottom, but it separated him from his rescuers all day Saturday, at the same time permitting them to talk to him with ease.

After the boy in Cave City told me that Floyd was trapped, I immediately sped toward Sand Cave. Many fears entered my mind. Would Floyd still be alive when I reached him? Would I find him crushed beneath tons of rock? Or was he merely sealed in temporarily by a blocking of the passage? Amid all these thoughts I kept repeating to myself, "If only I had stayed to help him when he asked me."

On arriving at Ed Estes' place, I parked my car on the side of the road and ran across the field. Never having been to the cave before, I did not know the exact location of the entrance. There were numerous people standing around, so I asked them where it was. They told me to follow the path down to the bottom of the bluff, and I ran down the hillside to the entrance.

The crowd of spectators was rapidly growing—sightseers who could see nothing, bystanders who got in the way and added to the confusion. Curiosity was beginning to play its terrible part. There were fifty to a hundred people standing around, and numerous campfires burning on top of the bluff. The snow that covered the ground was being melted by these fires, and the water was running over the bluff. There were icicles hanging from ledges.

When I arrived at the entrance, I asked if Floyd had been removed from the hole yet. They informed me that he was still trapped, but that it was possible to talk with him. There was a lantern standing nearby, so I grabbed it and started in.

"You can't go in there with those good clothes on," someone yelled. "You'll tear them to pieces."

I was wearing a new suit that I had bought in Louisville. "Clothes don't make no difference," I replied. "That's my brother down there."

On entering the hole, I found that it made a vertical drop of about eight feet. From there it sloped steeply downward, and I proceeded feet first. The floor of the passage was covered with mud from the water that was running. I came to the first tight squeeze, and found many would-be rescuers who would not or could not get through it. There were about a dozen men in the passage in front of the squeeze. As I crawled past them, I asked if anyone had been to Floyd. Apparently none of them had. I noticed some whiskey bottles on the ledge and saw that a few of the men in the tunnel were drunk. The air was filled with cigarette smoke.

I wiggled through the squeeze and left these men behind. From the way the passage turned as it dropped down, I figured that it must be doubling back under itself. In one place it was shaped like a corkscrew. Finally I reached a level stretch of tunnel at the end of which was the pit leading down to Floyd. Oscar Logston, German Dennison, Louis

Brown, and my brother Marshall were working in this part of the tunnel. They were the only men I had encountered after leaving the first squeeze. Logston was at the top of the pit over Floyd, trying to enlarge the opening so he could get through. I shouted down, "Floyd, are you all right?"

"That's my old buddy Homer," he said. "I knew you'd be coming down to help me. I'm not hurt, but my left leg is caught in a crevice. Watch out for loose rocks up there. My head is right at the bottom of the pit you have to come down through."

The others had not been able to squeeze through, and no one had been down to where they could reach Floyd up to that time. I was the same size as Floyd, so I figured that if he could get down, I ought to be able to. Oscar told me that he did not think I could make it. I still had my suit on, so I backed up to a spot where there was room enough to sit up and began taking it off. I stripped down to my underwear and even removed my shoes before starting down into the pit. I left my lantern at the top to be lowered down to me after I reached the bottom. It was very difficult to get through this hole because of the sharp, jutting rocks. The tight squeeze was bad enough, but the rock dug into my flesh as I forced my way through, going down feet first. As I neared the bottom, I began to feel around with my feet, and I shuddered as my feet came down on Floyd's head. There was barely room enough to crouch in the barrel-sized cubbyhole into which his head protruded. I called up for the lantern, which was lowered to me on the rope that Floyd had fastened in the tunnel up above.

When the lantern arrived, I saw for the first time how completely helpless Floyd was. His face was lying against a rock that pressed his nose to one side. Both of his arms were pinned in the crevice alongside his body so he could not use his hands, which were completely out of sight. Gravel and mud had poured into the crevice around his body. He was lying on his left side, turned somewhat on his back. Water was dripping steadily on him from above, and there was no way for him to avoid it. His lantern was lying there in front of him with the globe broken. "How come your lantern is up here and your hands are caught at your side that way?" I asked.

"I pushed it through first," he said, "before trying to get through myself. If you can dig away some of this gravel and enlarge the crevice, I'll have my hands free. It's my left foot that's caught by a rock. Once I get it free, I can get out of here."

I began removing the gravel from around his body. There was no place to dispose of the rocks, so I told them up above to bring down some sort of small bucket that could be used to raise the material out of the pit. They passed the word along the tunnel to the outside.

It was Saturday night and Floyd had been in the cave since early Friday morning with nothing to eat. "I'm awfully hungry," he said.

I yelled up to Oscar Logston to send out for some food. The word was again relayed along the tunnel. Ed Estes had his wife prepare some food for Floyd. About an hour after the message was sent, the food arrived. There were nine sausage sandwiches and a pint bottle of coffee. Despite all the rock that I had removed while waiting for the food to arrive, Floyd still could not get his hands to his mouth. I held his head up for him and placed the food in his mouth. That strange meal was like a feast to Floyd. I crouched there holding his head away from the rock, feeding him like a baby. He had lost a great deal of energy and was very hungry. It was obvious that he was in pain and his strength diminishing, but in spite of his suffering, he did not complain. I could not help crying. After feeding him, I dug furiously, piling gravel at my side in the cubbyhole. A one-gallon syrup bucket was lowered to me after a while. I filled the bucket with loose rock that I had dug away from around Floyd's body. Oscar Logston pulled it up and dumped it in the hole twenty feet away, where Floyd had first dug before trying the one in which he was stuck.

"I can move my right foot a little," Floyd said. "I've worked the boot off my right foot, but I can't get to the other one. If I didn't have that heavy boot on, I believe my left foot would slide through."

I continued digging the gravel away from around his body. It seemed that as fast as I removed it, more kept sliding in. Meanwhile, Floyd remained perfectly calm.

"It's a venturesome thing to explore," he said. "I guess we're all subject to it."

"Did you find anything down there?" I asked.

"Oh my, yes." he said. "I've been in big cave, but there's no formations. It looked to me like the walls were smoked. But if ever I get out of here, I'm never going back in it again."

The icy water dripping steadily on his face was maddening. No matter how he turned he could not avoid it. "Where's all this water coming from?" he asked. "It was not nearly so wet when I came in here."

"It's from the snow melting outside," I said. "There's a big crowd of people around the bluff and they have bonfires. I suppose the water is running over the bluff into the cave."

"The way that water is coming in," Floyd said, "I'm afraid it's going to fowl up the tunnel that I dug. It will have to be timbered up to keep from caving in."

I remembered that one side of the tunnel was solid rock while the other was loose material from the talus. When Floyd dug through this tunnel, it was dry, and there was very little danger of the wall caving in. Furthermore, since he had been the only one using the tunnel, there had been no one blundering up against the loose wall, making it unsafe by dislodging the rocks. But now it was wet, and with so many inexperienced people passing through, there was considerable danger of a slide blocking the tunnel. Already the floor of the tunnel had been converted into an ooze of mud and gravel.

Floyd had used a number of burlap sacks to tow material out of the tunnel as he dug through. I wrapped these around him in order to protect him from the ever-increasing flow of water. I covered as much of his body as possible, punching the burlap sacks into the crevice around his shoulders, and covering his face. He was greatly relieved to be free of the icy drip that had tortured him for so long.

I had been in the cave for eight hours trying to free Floyd. He wanted me to go out and rest, as I was cold, wet, tired, and bruised. But my own discomfort was small compared to his. Finally, I became too exhausted to work anymore. My fingers were skinned from digging with my bare hands. Being only in my underwear, I was shivering violently.

"You had better leave, Homer," Floyd said. "See if you can get Johnnie Geralds. He can help me. And try to get John Adwell and Dave Johnson, too." All three of these men were experienced in exploring caves. "And when you come back bring an oilcloth down to keep this water from dripping on me," he said as I was leaving.

Oscar Logston helped me out of the pit up into the tunnel. I put my clothes on again and returned to the surface. When I came out of the cave, it was Sunday morning. Although I had spent eight hours trying to release Floyd, both of his arms were still pinned in the crevice. I had removed a couple of bushels of gravel from around him with my bare hands, but more had slid in. At any rate, he was resting more comfortably than before, and he had received some food. My new suit was muddy and torn. I changed into some old clothes and got a pair of shoes from German Dennison to replace the dress shoes I was wearing.

That Sunday morning, I was nearly hysterical. There were many people standing around at the entrance just looking on. I screamed at them to get out of the way if they could not help. It was no use; they paid no heed to me.

The news of Floyd's entrapment had spread rapidly. Newspaper reporters began to arrive on the scene. They asked me about Floyd, and I told them they could find out by going down where he was trapped. It made me furious to see these curiosity seekers standing idly around while Floyd was down there suffering. The reporters cornered everyone who came out of the cave, and they received many conflicting stories, most of them from men who had never been past the first squeeze.

On Sunday afternoon, Mrs. Emmons Blaine, whom Floyd had guided through Crystal Cave the

The entrance to Sand Cave. *Photo from Howard W. Hartley's* Tragedy of Sand Cave.

previous summer, called from Chicago asking to speak to one of the Collinses. Like many other tourists, she had taken a liking to Floyd. I talked to her over the telephone at Bee Doyle's house. She asked if there was any way that she could help, if there was anything we needed for the rescue that she might send. "What we need is some daredevils to go down there and help get Floyd out," I said.

She told me that she would send a doctor to the scene to give any medical assistance that might be needed. Doctor William Hazlett arrived in Cave City by plane the next day.

Many men went into the tunnel that Sunday. Most of them never got close enough to Floyd to talk to him. Some of them were physically incapable, others did not even try. But they came out of the cave with wild stories to feed the waiting reporters. One man stated that he had been to Floyd and found him dead. This was quickly refuted by one of the rescuers who was known as Tennessee. When Tennessee went in and found that Floyd was still alive, the man who told the lie hastily disappeared.

The final squeeze just above Floyd's head was so narrow that only a small man could reach him. I weighed one hundred and sixty pounds and was just barely able to get through. I needed some small, wiry men who could work in the cramped space where Floyd was trapped to dig through to reach the rock that was pinning his foot.

Outside the cave there was nothing but confusion. I tried to organize a crew to work in shifts down in the hole next to Floyd, as one man could not work there effectively for any great length of time. I had no success in organizing such a party. After awhile, I gave up in disgust, deciding to go back in by myself rather than waste any more precious time.

In the meantime, amid all the confusing reports coming out of the cave, Marshall offered a reward of five hundred dollars to any one who would go down next to Floyd and find out for sure if he was still alive. Someone went into the cave, taking up Marshall's offer, and returned shortly afterward saying that it had caved in. He claimed that the passage was blocked and Floyd could not be reached. I knew that a few rocks might have fallen, but not enough to make it impassable. I was thoroughly disgusted with the reports of all these men who knew nothing of caves and were merely contributing to the general confusion. "I'm going in and find out the facts," I said to Marshall.

It was late Sunday afternoon when I entered the cave for the second time. Some rocks had fallen, but there was no cave-in. The passage was still open.

The rocks had probably been knocked loose by the passing of so many people who had carelessly brushed against the loose wall. I went down to Floyd and once again started digging around his body. He seemed to be in pretty good condition in spite of the fact that he had been in the cave for three days. His hopes were high. I noticed that the water was dripping in faster than ever, making the rescue work more difficult. I placed an oilcloth over him to shield his head from the maddening drip, and fed him again. There was a crowbar lying in the tunnel that he had used while working in the passage. "If you can slide that crowbar into my hand," Floyd said, "I believe I can get my foot loose."

His arms were still pinned at his side. The crowbar had to be poked into the crevice alongside his body until he could obtain a grip on it. In this way I placed it in his hand, and he began working on the rock above his foot. Every movement pained him. He tried as best he could to dislodge the rock, but his awkward position, the lack of space, and his weakened condition were all against him. He finally gave up the attempt.

I had decided to try and chip away the rock above him to make room enough to squeeze over his body and reach his legs. The boulder directly above him weighed several tons; it was solid limestone. I had carried a ball-peen hammer and a chisel down with me to chip away the rock. I started to work on it, but Floyd stopped me.

"That boulder is just wedged in there, Homer, and if you hammer on it, it may move. I'm afraid that if you jar that rock it will crush me." I gave up that plan and tried again to remove the gravel from around his body. Not having slept for a couple of days, I was completely exhausted.

I cannot blame those who did not reach him, for I do not believe I would have done it myself had anyone else been in there. For those who did reach him and tried to save him, I have the greatest admiration. When it became evident that I was not going to be able to get him loose on that trip, he made a request. "I'm awfully cold, Homer. I believe that some bitters like Mother used to make would help me out. Now don't get me any moonshine," he said, "I want some good stuff."

"I'll do my best, Floyd," I said.

I had spent about eight hours again on this second trip into the cave. I left him, promising to bring him a toddy the next time. When I returned to the surface, it was Monday morning. Floyd had been in the cave three days. I wondered how much longer he could hold out.

There were more newspaper reporters gathered around the entrance. By this time, I could not stand the sight of reporters or curiosity-seekers. Men had been running in and out of the tunnel telling the reporters that Floyd was dead, that he was alive, that he was still trapped, that he was free, that the tunnel had collapsed. And all the while they were making the rescue efforts more difficult. A small, thin fellow approached me as I was drying off from my trip in the cave. "I hear you are the brother of the fellow who is trapped in the cave," he said.

I looked him over. "I judge you're another reporter."

"Yes, I'm from the *Courier-Journal* in Louisville."

This slender young fellow was William Burke "Skeets" Miller, who later won a Pulitzer Prize for his coverage of the story. He was unknown then and, to me, just another pesky newsman. "Now if you want some information about this thing," I told him, "there's the hole right over there. You can go down and find out for yourself."

To my surprise he accepted the challenge. As he was getting ready to go into the cave, I advised him how to proceed, but he was too excited to pay any attention to me. I followed him a short distance into the tunnel, then came back out. Skeets was extremely small, so he had no great difficulty in getting past the tight squeezes. He managed to reach Floyd's side and saw for himself what the situation was. At last a reporter could give the world a first-hand account of the situation. This was most fortunate, as there had been so many false stories given out. Skeets was so impressed by Floyd's plight that he joined in the rescue work.

FIFTEEN

The Rescue Continues

Before entering the cave again, I had to fulfill my promise to Floyd and get him a toddy. On Monday, Oscar Logston and I drove to Cave City. There was no liquor being sold legally, except at drug stores where it could be obtained for medical purposes with a doctor's prescription. Oscar managed to get a half a pint of whiskey, and I bought some rock candy to mix in with it. By this time Floyd had been exposed to the dampness and cold for so long that I was afraid his throat would not stand a straight drink. Therefore I intended to weaken it so that it would take effect and yet go down smoothly.

We rushed back to the cave, where an enormous crowd was now gathered. Cars were parked bumper to bumper alongside the road and in the fields nearby. Oscar had the whiskey bottle in plain view as we approached the cave entrance, for we had no reason to hide it. I was trying to get some sort of container to mix the toddy in before taking it down to Floyd. While we were thus engaged, a deputy sheriff named Turner happened to see Oscar holding the whiskey. He confiscated the bottle, which was still sealed. "There's not going to be any whiskey going down there," Turner said.

I quickly explained to him that Floyd had requested it, but he would not give it back. At this I could no longer control my temper. Having promised Floyd that I would bring him a drink, I was determined to carry out that promise. "My brother is down there in the ice water and mud," I said, almost in tears. "He called for this and he's going to get it."

He still refused and I was furious.

"You're suppose to be the law. Why don't you get these people away from here? Look how their campfires are melting the snow. The water is running over the bluff into the cave, and Floyd is down there helpless. We're trying to do something for him. These people are hurting him."

My plea was useless. Turner was determined to stop the drinking that had gotten out of hand around the cave. He was merely doing his duty, but at the time I could not see it that way.

Oscar said to me, "Homer, you know I can't get through that last squeeze, but I'll stay up in the tunnel and help you all I can. Maybe we can get enough rock out of there to free Floyd."

Oscar and I went into the cave immediately. The old bucket we had been using was badly battered, so we got a new one to replace it. A one-gallon syrup bucket was about the largest container that could be hauled up through the tight squeeze above Floyd's head. We fastened a wire around the bucket for extra strength. This time we took a blowtorch in with us to work on the huge boulder that formed the ceiling of Floyd's prison. Limestone will crumble to pieces under intense heat. Old Jonathan Doyle, a Negro slave, had opened the entrance to nearby Proctor's Cave in this way. He had built a fire on the limestone rocks at a point where a draft of air issued from a crevice, thus discovering a large and beautiful cave. My intention was to break up the rock that hung over Floyd in the same manner. I thought that it could be done without burning him and without causing the entire boulder to fall. If the rock were to jar loose and shift the least bit, he would be instantly crushed to death. I hoped to crumble the bottom part away by concentrating the heat in a small area.

Oscar and I went into the cave with high hopes of success. When we reached Floyd, I scrambled down through the squeeze to Floyd's side, while Oscar remained at the top in the tunnel, ready to haul out the loose rock. I told Floyd of my plan to use the blowtorch and he agreed to let me try. Crouching in the cubbyhole next to Floyd's head with a blowtorch in my hand, I tried to light it, but it would not work. For quite some time I worked with it, trying to get the thing started, but with no success. Finally I gave up in despair. "This thing just won't work," I said. "We'll have to dig."

Time was so precious down there that I could not afford to waste a minute. I began digging without further delay. Floyd did not say much and I was too tired to talk. But as I worked in silence, another voice echoed through the narrow crevice. It was Oscar Logston in the tunnel above us praying for Floyd's release. He prayed in a loud voice, "O God, help us to save this man!"

I filled the bucket time after time. Oscar hauled it up, dumped the rocks, and sent the bucket back down to me. By removing enough material from under Floyd, I hoped to lower his body to a point where I could reach over the top of him. It was very difficult because of the fact that his body took up all the space, leaving no room in which to work. I could not reach past his shoulders. And always more gravel kept shifting in.

Oscar continued praying, "O God, help us save this man!"

Floyd said nothing. I worked as Oscar prayed, trying not to think. Floyd had always stressed the idea that caves were the work of God, that they showed His handiwork through nature. It was now beginning to look to as if only God's help could save him.

In all this time, Floyd never doubted that we would be able to free him. He had the greatest faith and boundless patience. He was calm all the time, cooperating in every way with our efforts. He was always concerned over our safety and comfort; he never complained about his own.

I worked desperately at removing the gravel from around him. Slowly the results began to show. After I had removed enough gravel from beneath him, his body gradually lowered in the crevice until there was enough room to reach over the top of him. Soon, I was able to get past his shoulders. At last, I had enough space to see his hands. The flesh was torn from his fingers where he had been clawing at the rocks. I shuddered at the grisly sight. Then I turned my eyes away and began digging again. Floyd told me that he thought his foot might be free. Perhaps it was numb and the lack of feeling gave him this impression. He suggested we tie a rope around his body and try pulling him out. This sounded like a good idea to me, for now I had removed enough material from the crevice to make it possible to fasten a rope around his chest. I decided to have a harness made to slip around his chest. With a rope attached to the harness, several men could pull from up in the tunnel, and perhaps we would be able to release him. If we did pull him out in this way, it would undoubtedly mean a broken ankle and extreme pain, but anything was better than to leave him as he was. Before leaving him, I freed both of his hands; they had been pinned in the crevice alongside his body for four days.

Tuesday morning, I went to Cave City to get a harness that would fit around his chest. A shoemaker made one for me. It consisted of a wide leather belt with a ring on it for attaching a rope. I returned to the cave with the harness and gathered some men to help me pull Floyd out. Skeets Miller and Lieutenant Burden of the Louisville Fire Department followed me into the tunnel. I went down through the squeeze to attach the harness to Floyd, while the others stayed in the tunnel just above us, ready to pull on the rope.

When I reached Floyd, he was working with the crowbar trying to dislodge the rock above his foot. The few inches that I had lowered his body on my previous trip gave him enough freedom to use the bar himself. He was punching at the rock with all his strength, but after five days of lying on the wet rocks his strength was nearly gone. Furthermore, it was not just the one rock holding his foot in the crevice, but several others he had kicked loose when his right foot was free. Of course, if that one rock that formed such a perfect wedge over his left foot could have been moved, we could easily have set him free.

I explained our plan to Floyd, showing him the

harness that I intended to use. He told me to go ahead. The belt was strapped around him with some difficulty, and the rope was attached to the steel ring. Directly above us were Skeets Miller, Lieutenant Burden, Oscar Logston, and German Dennison. Farther up the tunnel there were several men whose names I can't recall. From my position next to Floyd, I shouted directions up to the others. We began to pull. The belt tightened as the men strained at the rope. It was difficult for them to find traction in the slimy mud. There was considerable friction on the rope where it passed over the right-angle turn from the tunnel into the crevice. But there were enough men hauling on the rope to overcome these disadvantages. Floyd's body moved. I could see that he was in great pain. It looked as though he were being torn apart. Finally he could stand it no longer and cried in agony, "Stop! I can't stand it! It's going to pull me in two."

I tried to stop them from hauling on the rope, but was not able to do it immediately. Floyd was suffering excruciating pain. "It's breaking my back. Stop them!" he pleaded.

I tried to keep them from hurting him any more by pulling on the rope against them. They finally heard me, and the rope slackened. Floyd was in agony. His body had moved forward a few inches, but his foot was still caught the same as before. It seemed that he had been stretched out. Floyd's cries of pain had completely unnerved me. The idea of pulling him out was given up. I left the harness on him and began digging. It seemed that the only way to release him without killing him was to enlarge the space around his body until a small man could crawl over the top of him and remove the rock.

I had been able to remove enough material to get past his shoulders and free his hands, so I figured that at the same rate it should not take too long to reach his legs. If we could merely keep a small man working next to Floyd at all times we would soon have him free. The problem was to find enough small men to keep the work going continuously, and, most importantly, to organize their efforts. The trouble was that each man had his own idea of how to go about effecting the rescue, and no single method was followed through. An organized effort in one direction was needed. There was too much confusion, too many new experts constantly arriving, each with his own plan, and too much curiosity cluttering the area with onlookers.

While I was digging next to Floyd, he said, "Homer, I kept hearing rocks falling down into the pit behind me. I believe there's a hole in the ceiling back behind my feet that those rocks are coming through. It must lead to the tunnel just above us. Maybe they can get to me that way. I remember seeing a hole up there when I first came in."

There was, in fact, a hole in the tunnel up above, although I had not noticed it up to that time. It was not large enough to get through, and it was being used as a handy disposal for the material that was being dug out of the crevice. "I don't know if we'll be able to get down through it." I said, "but we'll do something. We're going to get you out."

I was not anxious to work on that project myself, for I felt that I could do more good working next to Floyd. Time was running short, and I was afraid that it would be too late to start on a new project. The hole was very small and had been filled with rocks. It was about ten feet above him, and that would mean ten feet of digging through solid rock, assuming that it did come out behind him. Now that I could almost reach his feet, I did not want to change my approach. When I became too exhausted to continue digging, I arranged his cover to protect him from the water and headed for the surface. When I left the cave, I met Johnnie Geralds at the entrance. I told him about the hole that might possibly go down behind Floyd, suggesting that he might try working it out. My nerves were badly shaken by the last ordeal, my body was cut and bruised by sharp rocks, and lack of sleep was beginning to tell on me. I was on the verge of collapse, so they rushed me to the Dixie Hotel in Cave City where I was put under the doctor's care. I faintly remember someone warning me, "You had better stay out or there'll be another Collins boy trapped in there."

At the Dixie Hotel, my cuts were treated and I was ordered to rest. I had been in the hotel for about two hours when one of the reporters who was staying there told me that Floyd had been released. I immediately put on my clothes and slipped out of the hotel. There were no cars or wagons that I could use at that hour, so I went out on the road and hitchhiked over to the cave. There was still a large crowd at the entrance. I asked someone eagerly, "Have they brought Floyd out yet?"

"No."

"Well, are they bringing him out now?"

"They can't bring him out. He's still trapped."

"Then I'm going back in the cave again and get him out," I cried.

"There are quite a few men in the tunnel and you can't go in," the man said. "You are in no condition to be going in the cave. You're too weak. You'd better rest up for awhile if you want to do any good."

Dejectedly, I climbed back up the hill and lay down on a cot, wondering what to do next. The rumor that Floyd was free had come about in the following way. Skeets Miller had gone into the cave and found the passage just above Floyd blocked by a rock fall. He was able to shout to him, however, and Floyd yelled back that he was free. Skeets questioned him further, and Floyd admitted that he was still trapped. Why he told Skeets that he was free, I do not know. Perhaps he was afraid that his rescuers might give up hope and wanted to spur them on.

So far I have related only my own attempts to rescue Floyd, since this is first-hand information. There were, of course, literally hundreds of people who contributed their efforts. I cannot name them all, nor can I describe in much detail the contributions that they made. However there are a few outstanding facts that must be mentioned.

As I said earlier, Floyd asked me to get some of his trusted friends who were experienced cave men to help us. One man he asked for in particular was Johnnie Geralds. Johnnie heard about Floyd being trapped and arrived at the cave on Sunday night to see if he could be of assistance. Johnnie was not a small man, and he was told by some of the men around the entrance that he was too large to get past the squeeze. Therefore he did not go into the cave immediately, but stayed on the surface helping in every way he could. After our attempt to pull Floyd out with the harness failed, Magistrate T. G. Turner, who was more or less in charge on the outside, gave Johnnie permission to go into the cave if he wanted to. Without hesitating, Johnnie put on some old coveralls and entered the cave. He hurried past several men on his way in. Arriving at the first squeeze, he passed through it without too much difficulty. He continued into the corkscrew turn and beyond. There was only one man left in front of him, Lieutenant Ben Wells, head of the Mathematics Department of Ogden College in Bowling Green, Kentucky. Johnnie shouted to Wells, and Floyd heard his voice down below.

"That's Johnnie Geralds. He's my friend. Let him down here. He'll get me out." Johnnie went to the edge of the squeeze just above Floyd, but could not make it through on account of his size. He stayed in the passage up above and removed a tremendous amount of rock, as Lieutenant Wells testified. Floyd called for something to eat and Johnnie sent word up through the tunnel to bring down some milk. A bottle of milk was brought in after awhile. Geralds tied a string around it, then lowered the bottle down to Floyd. Unfortunately Floyd was unable to reach it. Johnnie continued working from above until he was exhausted. That was his first trip in the cave; he made many more after that, contributing in large measure to the total rescue effort. He became one of the leaders in the rescue work. Johnnie Geralds took charge of the work when he was in the cave because of his experience. He had explored with Floyd in the lower levels of Crystal Cave and had helped Floyd out of a tight spot once before.

From all over the country came a continual influx of so-called experts, well-intentioned men who were good in their fields, but had no knowledge of caves. Hard feelings developed between Geralds and some of these outsiders. Factions began to develop, and some harsh words were passed among the opposing groups. There were reports of threats among the rescue workers. The tension was high.

The most outstanding name to come out of the drama was Skeets Miller. He came as a reporter and emerged as one of the foremost rescue workers. With no knowledge of caves, he risked his life to save a man completely unknown to him. Skeets was made to order for the tight squeezes. His small body could slide with ease through the narrow crevices where more powerful men were helpless. It was Skeets who placed the electric light bulb next to Floyd on Tuesday night. Up to that time a lantern had been kept burning in the cubbyhole near Floyd's head. This light bulb, which Skeets put against Floyd's body, was to play an important part later on.

Skeets also figured prominently in the attempt to raise the rock off of Floyd's leg with a jack and a crowbar. After I had dug out enough rock to lower Floyd's body in the crevice far enough to where we could reach past his shoulders, Skeets tried out the plan. He carried an automobile jack into the cave at first, but found that it was too large. A small jack only four inches in length was then sent in from Cave City. Skeets took this one in and tried to use it. The jack was too small this time. Rather than waste any more time trying to find a jack that was just the right size, he decided to use blocks between the small jack and the crowbar. At that time, there were so many men in the tunnel that they were able to pass the necessary material down to him along a human chain. The blocks were sent down to him in this way, and Skeets put them in place. He began raising the rock. Just as it seemed that the plan was going to work, the blocks slipped. He made repeated attempts, but each one failed. He finally gave up the plan; there was not enough room to work the jack. Floyd had been so confident this plan would work that his spirit was badly shaken by its failure.

Meanwhile, the human chain in the tunnel was contributing to the collapse of the loose wall. The members of the chain were unwittingly closing the only path of rescue. Floyd himself had foreseen this possibility early in the struggle. The men who were cluttering the tunnel, gradually weakening the loose wall of the passage, should have been working to timber it up, but there was too much confusion.

At the entrance of the cave, Floyd's dog Obie kept constant vigil for his master. He would hardly eat, and numerous times I had to warn people not to pet him. He would lie there on the ground for a long time, then get up and walk over to the hole. Peering inside, he seemed to be asking, "Where is my master? What is keeping him so long?" He would stand there for awhile looking into the hole, then turn and walk slowly away. We could not get him to leave, and he was practically starving to death as he lay there waiting for Floyd. He was a one-man dog.

A small city had sprung up around the cave. The moonshiners were in their glory. Floyd was trapped on Friday. By Monday the area began to take the atmosphere of a carnival, with much drinking, cursing, and fighting in the area around the cave. Irresponsible people went into the tunnel with great fanfare, stayed for a short while just out of sight, then returned with wild tales of conditions inside the cave. The food they were to carry to Floyd was later found on ledges all along the passage. The air was filled with rumors. Someone said that there was no one trapped in the cave at all, that the whole thing was just a publicity stunt.

The carnival atmosphere around Sand Cave. *Photo from Howard W. Hartley's* Tragedy of Sand Cave.

In Cave City, five miles away, people arrived by the thousands on their way to visit the cave where Floyd Collins was trapped. The hotels were filled and prices skyrocketed. The road leading in from Cave City was lined with automobiles. Crowds of people wandered along the road and through the fields. Moonshine was plentiful and drinking was in the open. There was no law.

On top of the bluff overlooking the cave entrance and in the fields there around, dozens of large campfires burned. The melting snow found its way into the cave. The passage became muddier. The loose wall became weaker. Fools and drunks blundered through the passage, speeding the work of the water. Far beneath the ground, a million miles removed from this, Floyd prayed in silence.

The cave, which had been just another hole up to that time, received its name during the rescue work. It was called Sand Cave. Actually this name was misleading, since it gave the impression that the cave was developed in sandstone. It is true that there was sand rock at the entrance and some sandstone inside the tunnel, but the cave itself was in limestone. The walls of the passage where Floyd was trapped were limestone; the pit that lay beneath him had limestone walls; it was a limestone rock that had wedged his foot in the crevice. There was no more reason to call this cave Sand Cave than any of the others in the region. All of them lie beneath the sandstone caprock. (The caves that have been commercialized are perfectly safe. No tourist need ever have the slightest fear in any of them.)

Suggestions poured in through the mail telling us how we should go about getting Floyd out of the hole. They seemed ridiculous to anyone who had been down to him, but they illustrated the confused thinking that prevailed and the faulty conception of the cave that most people had. They could not understand why we didn't go in with a drill and dig past him until we could lift the rock off his leg. Those who realized that the passage was extremely small in diameter made the mistake of over-simplifying the picture. They imagined it like a pipe. Only those who actually reached Floyd were able to understand the difficulties involved. It was a peculiar situation, a combination of many factors, all of which were working against us. The icy water, the mud, the knife-edged rocks, the tight squeezes, the twisting tunnel, the huge boulder above Floyd's body that threatened to crush him if it were jarred, the danger of a collapse in the tunnel, the shifting gravel that surrounded his body—these were some of the conditions that had to be overcome. It looked hopeless, but Floyd would not give up.

It was suggested that Floyd's leg be amputated. One account had it that I offered a reward to any surgeon who would perform the operation. This is not true; I was never in favor of amputation. If there had been room enough to perform the operation, it would not have been needed. If we could have gotten to his leg to amputate it, then we could have moved the rock that was holding him. But it was not possible to climb over his body to reach his leg. That cold, muddy, dripping crevice was not much of an operating table. But suppose Floyd's leg were amputated. He would still have had to be dragged out of the cave. It was difficult enough for a healthy man to crawl out under his own power. To pull a man out who was unconscious, with a bleeding stump of a leg dragging over the rocks and mud, would have meant certain death. There was only one way to save Floyd, which was to get at the rock that was holding his foot.

SIXTEEN

THE SHAFT

There had been a great deal of talk about sinking a shaft. I was opposed to the idea on the grounds that it would take too much time. Furthermore it would be necessary to blast, causing the loose rock in the tunnel to fall in. I was sure that Floyd could not stay alive for as long as it would take them to reach him. The shaft would have to be sunk lower than his body to be of any value. Those who favored the shaft claimed that it could be dug in a few days. Granting that this was possible, I argued that the blasting might cause a fatal rockfall. Johnnie Geralds was also opposed to the idea. The chief exponents of the shaft were mostly men who had not been down to Floyd.

It was a crucial time, for now we were almost able to reach the rock that was holding him. I tried to have the area cleared of spectators who were impeding the rescue work and melting the snow, but got no results. I wanted to have the tunnel timbered up to prevent its collapse before Floyd was freed. This would not be too difficult to do provided they did not wait too long. Once the loose wall began to cave in, it might be too late.

Tuesday evening, the general manager of the Kentucky Rock Asphalt Company, an engineer by the name of Carmichael, arrived at the cave and began to study the situation. Wednesday morning, three hundred troops of the National Guard arrived. They had been called in to maintain order among the wild crowd that surged around the entrance. I was about to make another trip into the cave when several troops surrounded me. "Don't try to go into the cave," they warned me.

"My brother is in there," I said. "You can't keep me out."

They did keep me out in spite of my protests. I was nearly crazy with worry, for I knew that Floyd must be released quickly if he was to be brought out alive. The increasing talk of sinking a shaft had me worried, since it was almost sure to block the tunnel. I kept thinking to myself, "By the time they reach him, he'll be dead." Now that Carmichael was on the scene, the shaft plan gained strength, and many people rallied to his side. I fought the idea, but there were too many against me, too many surface superintendents who had never been past the squeeze. I saw Skeets Miller Wednesday, and he informed me that he had been down to see Floyd since my last trip. "Floyd's resting nicely," he said. "I've put an electric light by him."

I was very glad to receive this news, but the turn of events on the surface overshadowed the good news. Johnnie Geralds had been accused of obstructing the rescue work. It appeared to me that he was one of the most faithful and hard working men to enter the cave, but the accusation aroused suspicion.

Carmichael, the engineer who supervised the digging of the shaft. *Photo from Howard W. Hartley's* Tragedy of Sand Cave.

Johnnie naturally resented the interference of newcomers who were long on ideas and short on experience. Nerves were on edge and tempers were short. The basis for the accusation against Johnnie seemed to be his previous business dealings with Floyd regarding Crystal Cave. He had been negotiating with Floyd and my father to obtain an option on the cave. Of course Floyd would not come to terms as quickly as Pap, having great faith in the value of Crystal Cave. He expected it to be one of the foremost tourist attractions some day. Then, too, Crystal Cave was his greatest discovery. Nevertheless, Johnnie and Floyd got along very well together. Their business dealings had nothing to do with their personal relationship. That they were good friends was evident from the fact that Floyd took Johnnie exploring with him into the lower levels of Crystal Cave.

On Wednesday afternoon, it was reported that the tunnel was blocked. This time the report was not merely a fabrication of some publicity seeker. There had actually been a cave-in in the passage. Just when it appeared that rescue was at hand, nature prevented it. However, the fault was not entirely nature's, as the human chain that lined the tunnel had contributed as much as anything else to the cave-in. So many men had entered the cave, and so few had ever gone anywhere close to Floyd. If only those men would have spent their time bracing the wall of the tunnel.

The report of the collapse swung the weight in favor of digging a shaft. Lieutenant Governor Harry H. Denhardt arrived Thursday and lent his backing to the decision. He was Brigadier General of the Kentucky National Guard. I remember him saying, "Practical men have had their day; it takes men with brains to get him out. We'll sink a shaft."

I argued with him. "You can't sink a shaft through this formation and get him out alive. We've got to timber out the bad places inside the passage and get all these damn fools out of here." Denhardt ordered me away.

Carmichael sent his man into the tunnel to survey it in order to locate the site of the shaft. One of

Floyd's brothers Homer and Marshall during the rescue attempt. *Photo from the Ernst Kastning Collection.*

these men, Roy Hyde, claimed that he got close enough to talk to Floyd. He says Floyd answered his shouts through the debris. "You're too slow."

The shaft was begun on Thursday afternoon, February 5, 1925. I felt that this made the possibility of rescue more remote than ever, but Floyd had never lost faith, and I did not want anyone else to give up hope.

On Friday, Johnnie Geralds asked Carmichael, who was then in charge of the operation, to let him go into the cave. He was refused. Later in the day I slipped past the guards and entered the tunnel with a flashlight. It had been reported that the first squeeze was closed. This was not true, for I went past that point without any trouble. Farther down, I encountered some loose rock that was blocking the passage, but this could have been removed very

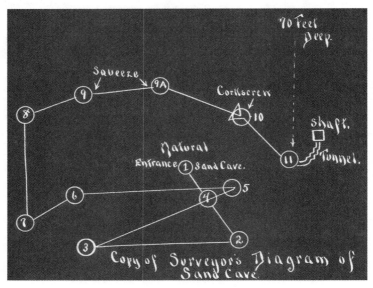

Surveyor's diagram of Sand Cave.
CRF Collection.

easily. Any moment, I feared that a dynamite blast might be set off by the crew working on the shaft. I did not want to be trapped myself by any rock fall resulting from such a blast. Nevertheless I stayed, calling to Floyd, and listening intently for an answer. It seemed to me that I could hear him through the debris. Whether it was Floyd or not, I cannot say for sure. Under such conditions, alone in a cave, you can hear anything you listen for.

In the meantime, my absence was noticed on the surface. The National Guard discovered that I had slipped into the cave, and two of them came in after me. I was already on my way out when I met them. One of them said to me, "Don't you know that you can be court-martialed for this?"

"I don't give a damn about you and your martial law," I answered. "My brother is down there dying, and I was trying to help him." They warned me not to try and go into the cave anymore, then let me go. I met Johnnie Geralds and a few others, and told them that the squeeze was not closed up as had been reported, that there were some loose rocks in the way that could easily be removed. Of course, when they started blasting in the shaft, it would really become blocked.

"I knew the hole wasn't closed up." Johnnie said. "I don't care who said it, even if Denhardt did himself."

While we were talking, the Lieutenant Governor had walked up behind Johnnie. At this remark Denhardt grabbed Geralds by the arm and said, "Get out of here and don't come back."

Johnnie was barred from the rescue area. All hope of working on the tunnel was gone. From now on Floyd's life depended on how quickly the shaft could be dug. Although I had been against the idea of sinking a shaft, now that it was started I gave them my support and prayed that they would reach Floyd in time.

With the abandonment of the tunnel, no one knew for sure if Floyd was still alive. However, there was one development that kept up our hopes; this was the celebrated "radio test." The light bulb Skeets Miller had taken into the cave was resting against Floyd's body. H. G. Lane, a radio enthusiast, conceived the idea of detecting any motions in the bulb by means of electronic apparatus hooked onto the other end of the wire at the surface. As Floyd breathed, the bulb would be moved, and these motions should show up on the apparatus. The equipment was brought in and the tests were begun. The signals were picked up and analyzed by Doctor Hazlett to determine whether or not Floyd was still breathing. Doctor Hazlett concluded from the rate at which the signals were received that they represented Floyd's breathing movements. In one report, the frequency was about twenty-two to twenty-six cycles per minute. This was slightly faster than normal, but that was to be expected in his condition. It also showed that he was not suffering from pneumonia, for in that case the number of breaths per minute is about fifty. This news was very heartening in view of the fact that so many people feared he would certainly die of pneumonia before he was freed.

The reports from the radio test were like cries for help, spurring the men on when all seemed hopeless. The value of those tests has been questioned. Many argue that they could not have detected Floyd's breathing. The experts were in disagreement on this matter, but the fact remains that the tests were a great morale builder for the rescue workers. It was hoped that another way might be found into the cave. Banana oil was sprayed into the tunnel in an attempt to discover some other means of entry. Perhaps there was another opening somewhere nearby that would lead into the cave; if so, it could be detected by the odor of the banana oil. The test proved unsuccessful—no new entrance was found. All hopes were now centered on the shaft.

SEVENTEEN

The Inquiry

As the entire civilized world waited for the news of Floyd's release, the throng of reporters around the cave hunted for any bit of news to send out. Any rumor or suspicion floating among the crowd was immediately pounced on and fed to the press. Some of the people who lived nearby—people who had never been into the cave—started a rumor that threatened the entire rescue effort. They said that Floyd was not really trapped and that the whole affair was just a publicity scheme to attract tourists. They claimed the whole affair was a hoax. This hoax story was sent out by a reporter and hit the headlines of the papers throughout the nation.

The public was roused. If the rumor was true, it was the biggest, most gruesome hoax that could have been imagined. Of course, there was not a particle of truth in the story, but it raised doubts in the mind of the public. Some people suspected that Floyd had another entrance to the cave, a back door through which he could leave whenever it was convenient. Many thought he was not in the cave at all. We who had been down past the squeeze were disgusted. The governor of the state of Kentucky, William Jason Fields, ordered that an inquiry be held to get at the truth and dispel these rumors.

Another reason for holding the inquiry was to investigate the charges against Johnnie Geralds. Accused of hindering the rescue and ordered off the scene by Denhardt, Johnnie was looked at with suspicion by the public. It was necessary to clear these matters up immediately, and so a military inquiry was started on Monday morning, February 9, 1925. It was held in Cave City, with Lieutenant Governor Denhardt in charge. Skeets Miller was the first to testify.

Question: I will ask you to describe to the court your journey through the cave, what you saw, and all that happened.
Answer: Well, I went in on my hands and knees for, I should say, about twenty feet, where the passage becomes so narrow that you are forced to get down on your stomach and move yourself along with your elbows.
Question: What weight are you Mr. Miller?
Answer: About one hundred ten, now, sir. I am usually around one hundred twenty, but I am a little bit light right now. The cave is very twisted, turns a lot, and the roof has a lot of big rocks in it, and smaller ones that are just stuck up there and look like they might fall. I don't know anything about caves, but I could see from the condition there that we were in a place that might be dangerous. I went on in front and made the squeeze all right. I didn't have any trouble and didn't stick in any of the tight places, and went until, before I real-

ized it, I was right on top of Floyd. When we got to within, I should say, ten feet of him, I began calling, "Floyd! Floyd!" All the answer I got was a sort of a groan, just an "uh uh," and knew then that someone was down there. I slipped going down this so-called chute and landed right on top of him almost before I realized I had come to him. I twisted down until I was right at his face and found that somebody had been there and covered his head with some sort of cloth—like oilcloth—that went on down over part of his body.

Question: Someone had covered over with a cloth?

Answer: Yes, sir, there was an oilcloth over his head and face.

Question: Did you receive any information there from him as to when the first person had gone back to him in the cave?

Answer: No, sir, at that time I did not.

Question: Did you later?

Answer: Yes, sir. I learned from Floyd on one of the three trips Tuesday evening that his brother had been in there to him and had fed him.

Question: What was your information as to when this occurred?

Answer: I believe he said he was fed Saturday evening.

Question: That was the next day after he was hung in the cave?

Answer: Yes, sir, and he also said that Geralds had been down there digging and moving rocks from around him.

Later:

Question: Did he say what size cavern that was?
Answer: No, he never told me that.
Question: Mr. Miller, from your conversation and talk with him, was he at himself the first time you talked to him, or not?
Answer: He was in a stupor that morning. He wanted to be left alone.
Question: Was he rational in all your other conversations with him?
Answer: Yes, sir. On Tuesday he said himself, "I'm at myself now."
Question: That was Tuesday?
Answer: Yes, sir.
Question: And you say you talked to him about another opening to the cave?
Answer: Yes, sir. He said there were none.

Later in his testimony Skeets answered some questions concerning Johnnie Geralds:

Question: Were you ever in there—in the cave—with Mr. Geralds?
Answer: No, sir, I don't believe we ever made a trip together.
Question: You don't think you were ever in it at the same time he was?
Answer: No, sir, because he always led one party himself, and there was no use in two lead men going in with the same party.

Later:

Question: Was he [Johnnie Geralds] ever in there with Lieutenant Burden?
Answer: I don't know, but I don't believe so. I know

that Geralds always picked his own men. I assumed that he did that because he knew the ones that knew the cave.

My father was called on to testify concerning the good intentions of Johnnie Geralds.

Question: You are perfectly satisfied with the work of Mr. Geralds?
Answer: Yes, sir. I feel that he did all that he could. He lay in the water and ice, and came out cramped from the cold. I had to rub him. Only he said there were enough sandwiches in the cave to feed the whole crowd. He said it was a shame.

Johnnie Geralds, the center of controversy, was called to the stand. Before he testified, the following statement was read in the court: "I wish to state that Mr. Geralds is represented by his attorney, C. H. Hatchett, and any statement that Mr. Geralds may make may be used against him, and that he will not be required to answer any questions only under his attorney's advice, and that you are expected to make only such statements as you are willing to make under the advice of your attorney in this court."

Question: You were acquainted with Floyd Collins?
Answer: Yes, sir.
Question: How long have you been acquainted with him?
Answer: Ever since I was a kid.
Question: Were you acquainted with Sand Cave?
Answer: No, sir.
Question: You have done a good deal of work in caves?

Answer: Well, a good deal, yes, sir.
Question: Did you have any business connection with Floyd Collins?
Answer: No, sir.
Question: Did you have any with his father?
Answer: Only an option on the cave was all.
Question: You have obtained an option on Crystal Cave?
Answer: Not at present.
Question: Had you had any before that time?
Answer: I have had a option in 1924.
Question: When did that option expire?
Answer: January 1, 1925.
Question: Did the option include part that was owned by him up to that time?
Answer: Yes, sir.
Question: Have you gotten a new option since then?
Answer: I just continued my option on Mr. Collins.
Question: Have you made any attempt to get an option on that part owned by Floyd Collins.
Answer: No, sir.
Question: What were your relations with Floyd Collins, pleasant or unpleasant?
Answer: Pleasant.
Question: Have you ever had any difficulties with him?
Answer: No, sir. Never in my life.

L. B. "Tennessee" Hooper, an electrician for the Louisville and Nashville Railroad, and a sincere rescue worker, gave the following testimony:

Question: What was being done there? [at Sand Cave]
Answer: I thought every thing was done that could

be done. They were trying to get a party to go in and it did not seem that anyone wanted to go; and there was some stranger there, and he said he would go in. This fellow went in—I had never had any experience in caves in my life, and I wanted someone to go in with me—and this stranger—I do not know his name—told me he would go in; and I got some overalls on, and about that time we started to go down to the first squeeze and they said I could not make it past there, but when we get down there, one of them said he could not make it, and I told him I believed he could, and he finally did. When he got down to where Floyd Collins was—I understood his name was Floyd—I heard him talking to his brother, Marshall, and we asked him how far we were from him, and he said about twenty-five or thirty feet. I tried to get in head first—you are supposed to go in feet first—and I kept on and looked into the hole. I had an idea that if I could get down there to where this drop is, that I could hang my feet around this rock and look in; but when I looked in I couldn't do nothing and I got pretty cold. I had a carbide light bumping my head every second and finally got out of the cave and said I was not going in there again. But I think Oscar Lawson [Logston] went in there about 3 or 4 o'clock, and I went in again about 7 o'clock to look around.

Concerning the man who had reported Floyd dead on Sunday, February 1, Hooper had this to say:

Hester wanted some money and Marshall said, "If you will go down there and bring me out a true report," he would pay him five hundred dollars; and then he turned to me and told me he would give me twenty-five dollars if I would go with him, and I told him he must think I was a damned fool to go in there and risk my life for twenty-five dollars. Hester went down there and came back and reported that he was dead—that he felt the cold sweat on his forehead, and that he heard him breathe his last breath—and I said, "I just don't believe it."

[Hooper went into the cave and refuted the story that Floyd was dead; Hester disappeared.]

Question: In your opinion—the last time you went in there—has anyone been doing anything about trying to construct a passage, and what was the spirit of the men that went in there?
Answer: It looked like everyone was doing all he could to get him out, and did everything in a spirit of kindness. They just couldn't get it, and they had to have some other way to get him out to get started.
Question: Do you mean that all these men, including Johnnie Geralds, were doing good work?
Answer: I thought it was mighty fine. He said he would stay with me as long as I stayed in the hole, and it looked to me like he had done everything a man could do, that he had done everything in the world a man could for that boy.

The military inquiry remained in session, issuing daily communiqués to the press. The hoax story was refuted, and Johnnie Geralds was cleared of charges against him.

EIGHTEEN

The Race Against Time

Those who thought the shaft would reach Floyd within a couple of days were badly mistaken. My own objection to digging the shaft had been that it would take too much time; this prediction was being borne out. The collapse in the tunnel had come suddenly, catching us unprepared, and there was no means of getting food to Floyd. If it had been anticipated, a tube could have been taken into him to feed him while the shaft was being dug. A telephone could have been placed by him to communicate with the outside world. As it was, he was without food or companionship, only the light bulb lying against his body to remind him of the world he had left behind.

In addition to Floyd being without food, another result of abandoning the tunnel was that the quilts that had been placed around his body could not be changed. The oilcloth might keep the water from dripping on his face, but the dampness was penetrating and he needed constant protection from the icy sweat of the rocks around him.

Floyd's sister, father, and two brothers wait at Sand Cave. *Photo from Howard W. Hartley's* Tragedy of Sand Cave.

The radio tests gave great encouragement to the men working in the shaft. These men were exposed to considerable danger themselves, but never faltered in their efforts. When it seemed as though the shaft might collapse, the men did not stop working; the side walls were timbered up, and the work went on day and night without let-up. There were more than enough volunteers, and many large corporations contributed to the rescue work. The L&N Railroad was particularly generous in sending material of all sorts, including expensive machinery. But with all the manpower and machinery available, it seemed as though we were helpless.

No one knows how many thousands of sightseers flocked to the area. There were several thousand automobiles standing in the vicinity. They were parked on both sides of the road, bumper to bumper, forming a line nearly ten miles long on the road between Mammoth Cave and Cave City. The troops of the National Guard helped keep order among this enormous crowd and prevented any interference with the rescue work.

As the shaft deepened, the work became increasingly hazardous. There was constant danger of falling rock or a collapse. In spite of these conditions, hundreds of volunteers continued to pour in from all over the country. A heavy rainstorm put the entire framework of the shaft in danger, but the work continued. Morale had to be kept high under such conditions, and the reports from the radio test supplied this demand. Those who had faith in the radio test claimed that it showed Floyd was still alive. The public was kept informed of the progress in the shaft and of the results of the inquiry day to day. Was Floyd still alive? Would they reach him in time? Time was the big factor—and it was running against him.

On February 11, a telegram was received from Haddam, Kansas, from a man who claimed that he

Digging the rescue shaft. *Photo by Russell T. Neville. CRF Collection.*

was Floyd Collins. "Please contradict statement that I am buried alive in Sand Cave. Tell Mother I am all right. Am coming home." The man was easily shown to be an impostor. His description did not fit, nor did he have sufficient knowledge of Floyd's life. Furthermore, Floyd's mother had been dead since 1915. Although the man was shown to be a fake, he revived the hoax story in many people's minds.

Before the shaft was sunk deep enough to reach Floyd from below, a lateral tunnel was started at the bottom of the shaft. This decision was made because of the difficulties involved in digging through the dangerous formation at that level. There was not time enough to get below him as they had first intended.

On Friday morning, February 13, a crew in the shaft broke into a hole on the side and found a crevice about five feet long. They shouted Floyd's name, but received no answer. One of the diggers asked if anyone had coughed. They listened, and William Bailey said that he heard the sound also—two coughs. None of the workers had coughed.

Ed Brenner, a miner from Cincinnati, went into the old tunnel that Floyd had used and proceeded as far as the breakdown that blocked the passage. He was going to exchange signals with the crew in the shaft. Bailey accompanied him as far as the first squeeze. Following is the testimony he gave at the inquiry concerning the result of that test:

Question: What did you do down there?
Answer: I went down to listen to the sound, see, the sound of our working, and I find out how far we are, and to give the boys a sound, the boys in the pit.

Question: Did you hear any sounds they made?
Answer: I certainly did.
Question: How far do you think it was from where you were to where the sounds were coming from?
Answer: The sound came ten feet from me, ten feet to my estimation. Yes, I think it is ten feet from where I was.
Question: Ten feet from where you were in the tunnel?
Answer: Yes, sir.
Question: How far back into the tunnel did you go?
Answer: I was at the place where it caved in.
Question: You saw the cave-in there, did you?
Answer: Why, certainly; I was at it.
Question: Did you hear any sound while you were down there?
Answer: How you mean? Our men working?
Question: No, any other sound? Did you hear anybody breathing?
Answer: Yes, I heard one deep—gasp—like this.
Question: A kind of loud, long breath?
Answer: It was something like a groan, but not a loud groan. Not a groan like you hear a man that gets hurt, in a hospital, you know.
Question: A gasp?
Answer: Yes, now you got it; now you got into my dictionary. If I brought my dictionary with me, I tell you a lot quicker. It was a gasp.
Question: Did you find some harness down there in the cave?
Answer: Yes, there was a harness there. I picked it up. It had some dirt on it, and I picked the dirt out a little, and they got it out there now.
Question: Where was this gasp you heard in rela-

tion to where you were? Was it in front of you?
Answer: Yes, it was in front of me. I couldn't hear no more and I hollered out, "Floyd! Floyd!" And Floyd don't answer, for he is where he can't, I guess. So I holler, "Hold out; we are coming."

Whether or not the sound the diggers heard was actually Floyd, I do not know. The report brought new hope to the exhausted workers, removing some of the fear that Floyd was already dead. It was expected that the tunnel would reach him within a few hours.

The lateral tunnel, which was being dug from the bottom of the vertical shaft to the cave, did not follow any natural crevice. It was being dug through the limestone. This tunnel was in grave danger of a collapse. It was timbered up and pushed on toward the cave passage. At 1:30 A.M. Monday, February 16, Carmichael announced that the lateral tunnel had been extended ten feet from the shaft. At the same time that this announcement was being issued, the men in the shaft were making the final discovery. A. Blevins was digging with a spade when he broke through the last bit of earth separating the lateral tunnel from the cave passage. Minutes later, Carmichael descended into the shaft. Ed Brenner was sent for, and the plucky miner scrambled into the hole that had been made. They waited tensely for his return. Five minutes later he came out with the somber announcement that Floyd was dead.

Carmichael returned to the surface to confer with the officials. An official statement was then released to the members of the press.

> At 1:30 o'clock, the lateral heading at a distance of twelve feet from the shaft, as

measured circularly, broke through into a natural cave just below the breakdown, which was found completely closed. This came after breaking through the four-foot ledge of rock, which verified the predictions to an inch. The distance from the entrance to Collins' head is six feet. The location of Collins is at the elevation originally estimated and within a few feet of the position detected by the first survey. First intimation of the old tunnel was the finding of several bottles, working tools, line of rope, wires, line of one-inch rope, and line of three-eighths rope. Mr. Carmichael was called in by Albert Marshall when these were found. In the shaft were Marshall, A. Blevins, Simon Johns, and John Stevens. Immediately after the development, Ed Brenner was called to hurry timber work, the old cavern being found in extremely critical condition. Later, Johnnie Geralds and Lieutenant Ben Wells, conspicuous in original cave rescue work, were called down to identify the articles found, and this definitely determined Collins' position. This check was necessary on account of the inadvisability of entering the opening until timber work was done. The articles and their position were positively identified. Meanwhile, Albert Marshall, showing the same splendid courage so manifest throughout the shaft work from surface to foundation, without thought of personal danger, propped the loosely hanging, dangerous boulders and let himself down into the pit feet foremost, the opening being too small on account of his large stature for him to go in head first. He touched with his feet what he thought to be the blanket around Collins. Immediately after this, his game little partner, Ed Brenner, whose work had been conspicuous and of untold value, by reason of his comparatively small stature, great strength, agility, and iron nerve, went down into the hazardous pit. With a light he closely examined face and position of the man we believe to be Floyd Collins, and called up to Mr. Carmichael, five feet above him, that the man was cold and apparently dead. From information at hand it will be several hours before a physician or anyone else can safely reach Collins, unless it develops that a way can be found of driving a shaft which will reach Collins' feet. It will probably be thirty-six hours before the body can be brought from the shaft.

Doctor Hazlett and Captain C. E. Francis, a medical officer in the National Guard, went into the shaft to examine Floyd's body to establish that he was dead beyond all question. The physicians were unable to reach him, but Brenner went in front of them and they gave him instructions as to what he should do. The examination was made in this way, and Floyd was officially declared dead.

The next problem was to get his body out of the hole. They had broken into the cave at the top of the squeeze just above Floyd, and so were no better off than we had been before the shaft was begun. As a matter of fact, the man-made tunnel was as dangerous as the cave itself. Floyd's foot was still held in the vise and no one could reach it. If his body was to be removed, the shaft would have to be sunk deeper in order to strike the cave below him. It was suggested that his leg be cut off, but I could not bear the thought of that. Now that all hopes of saving him were past, there was a general letdown in the spirit of the rescue workers. No one was willing to risk his life any longer to remove a corpse from the hole. The decision was made to fill up the shaft and let it be Floyd's final resting place.

The public had to be assured that there was no hoax, so someone had to go in and take a picture of Floyd before the shaft was filled. On February 17, John Steger, staff photographer of the Chicago *Tribune*, volunteered for the job. He went into the cave and found Floyd lying with his face turned upward and his left arm folded across his chest. There were no marks on his head except for a spot on the cheek undoubtedly caused by dripping water. The photo-

Abandoned shaft at Sand Cave. *Photo by Russell T. Neville. CRF Collection.*

graph was made and the shaft was sealed. Church service was held on top of the bluff. The crowd disappeared. The struggle was over.

NINETEEN

Floyd's Mausoleum

The house at Crystal Cave had been deserted during the weeks of rescue work, as the family had stayed at Sand Cave throughout the long struggle, waiting and praying for Floyd's release. I had been sleeping on a cot up on top of the hill, ready to enter the cave on a moment's notice. I looked like a scarecrow, with long beard and hair thickly matted with dirt from my last trip into the cave. When we returned to the house at Crystal Cave, it was something less than going back home. It could never be like home again. I was nervous and worried. I kept thinking of Floyd lying in the muck where he had suffered beyond our power to imagine. I would never have peace of mind if he remained there. He had to be brought out of the hole.

At about this time I received an offer from a theatrical agent to make personal appearances in theaters around the country, explaining to the public in my own words the Sand Cave tragedy. At first the idea seemed repugnant to me, but it was brought to my attention that the money could be used to open

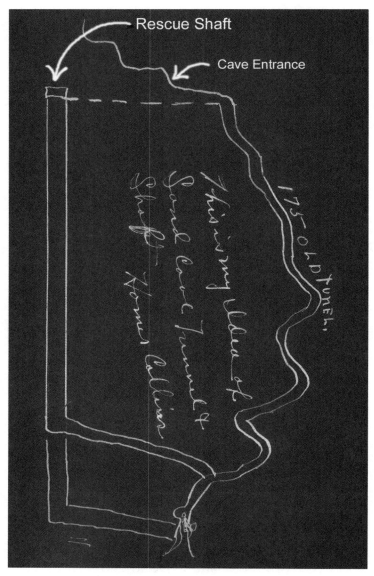

Sketch by Homer Collins of the rescue and recovery shaft at Sand Cave. *CRF Collection.*

the shaft and bring Floyd out for a decent burial. I therefore accepted the offer. I began a tour that started in Chicago and carried me all over the country. Oscar Logston, who had been of such great assistance in the early rescue work, accompanied me on the tour. We took Floyd's faithful dog, Obie, along with us. In St. Louis, Missouri, Obie got away from me. I had left him in the car while I went up to my hotel room. On returning, Obie was gone. I looked for him everywhere in the vicinity, but couldn't find him. I left the door of the car standing open in hopes that he would come back and climb inside. Then I went to the newspaper and posted a reward for him, but I never saw Obie again. To this day, I don't know what happened to him.

When I had finally earned enough money to begin work on the shaft, I returned to Kentucky to have Floyd's body removed. The original shaft was reopened and sunk twelve feet deeper. This time Floyd was approached from below. The rock that held his foot was found to weigh only about fifty pounds. Several other rocks had also fallen down around it. There were no broken bones. Floyd was brought out of the cave. He had been there for eighty-two days. He was taken to an undertaker's parlor in Cave City run by Johnnie Geralds' father and uncle. Floyd had some money in the bank at the time of his death, and with this money we bought a fine casket and a large steel vault. The casket was placed in the vault, and Floyd was buried on the hillside over Crystal Cave, just a short distance from the entrance. This would have been his final resting place, but another development soon occurred.

My father was very anxious to sell Crystal Cave. Doctor Harry Thomas, owner of Mammoth Onyx

Floyd's body with minister and recovery crew.
Photo by Wade Highbaugh. CRF Collection.

Cave, located about two miles from the town of Horse Cave, bought Crystal Cave for ten thousand dollars. After this, it was decided that Floyd was to be taken from his hillside grave and placed inside Crystal Cave. The grave was dug up and the steel vault was cut open. The casket was placed in the Grand Canyon inside the entrance of Crystal Cave, Floyd's great discovery.

I had no desire to live in the cave region any longer. The greatest explorer was gone, and old memories haunted me. I became restless. After wandering about the country for some time, I finally settled in Louisville. Time was slowly molding the past into a dream. Then one day a startling report came out of the cave region: Floyd's body had been stolen. Someone had broken into Crystal Cave during the night and taken his body out of the casket. Placing it inside a sack, the grave robbers dragged his body out of the cave and through the woods to the Green River bluff a few hundred yards away. They threw the body over the bluff, but it did not fall into the river. It was later recovered and returned to the casket inside the cave. The guilty parties were never caught. What could have been the reason for stealing his body? I don't know. It certainly could

Bee Doyle, who operated Sand Cave as a tourist attraction, holds the rock that trapped Floyd Collins. *Photo by Russell T. Neville. CRF Collection.*

not have been vengeance, for Floyd had never harmed anyone in his life.

Today [1955] Floyd lies in Crystal Cave. Around him the caving activities that he knew so well are still being carried on. His dream that the cave would some day become famous and worth a great fortune has come true. Even as I write, the government is trying to acquire it for inclusion within Mammoth

Lee Collins beside the grave of his son on the family farm in 1926. *Photo by Russell T. Neville. CRF Collection.*

A caver paying tribute to Floyd Collins on his way into Floyd's Great Crystal Cave.
Photo by Roger E. McClure.

Cave National Park, as it is one of the great natural wonders of our country.

The policy of the present management of Crystal Cave has been to promote further exploration as well as commercial development. Almost every week explorers tramp past Floyd's casket on their way to the lower levels—to Floyd's Lost Passage.

They wonder how many other passages in that great maze were explored by Floyd and never recorded, still waiting for another man of his daring nature to discover them. The tourists who daily visit the cave pause next to his casket as they view the impressive Grand Canyon Avenue. Here both tourist and explorer, wondering at the discoveries made single-handed, pay tribute to the great caver as they admire his greatest discovery—his mausoleum.